WITHDRAWN

NEW DIRECTIONS FOR STUDENT SERVICES

Margaret J. Barr, *Northwestern University*
EDITOR-IN-CHIEF

M. Lee Upcraft, *The Pennsylvania State University*
ASSOCIATE EDITOR

Making Enrollment Management Work

Rebecca R. Dixon
Northwestern University

EDITOR

Number 71, Fall

JOSSEY-BASS PU
San Francisco

MAKING ENROLLMENT MANAGEMENT WORK
Rebecca R. Dixon (ed.)
New Directions for Student Services, no. 71
Margaret J. Barr, Editor-in-Chief
M. Lee Upcraft, Associate Editor

Microfilm copies of issues and articles are available in 16mm and 35mm, as well as microfiche in 105mm, through University Microfilms Inc., 300 North Zeeb Road, Ann Arbor, Michigan 48106-1346.

LC 85-644751   ISSN 0164-7970   ISBN 0-7879-9976-8

NEW DIRECTIONS FOR STUDENT SERVICES is part of The Jossey-Bass Higher and Adult Education Series and is published quarterly by Jossey-Bass Inc., Publishers, 350 Sansome Street, San Francisco, California 94104-1342. Second-class postage paid at San Francisco, California, and at additional mailing offices. POSTMASTER: Send address changes to New Directions for Student Services, Jossey-Bass Inc., Publishers, 350 Sansome Street, San Francisco, California 94104-1342.

SUBSCRIPTIONS for 1995 cost $48.00 for individuals and $64.00 for institutions, agencies, and libraries.

EDITORIAL CORRESPONDENCE should be sent to the Editor-in-Chief, Margaret J. Barr, 633 Clark Street, 2-219, Evanston, Illinois 60208-1103.

Cover photograph by Wernher Krutein/PHOTOVAULT © 1990.

Manufactured in the United States of America. Nearly all Jossey-Bass books, jackets, and periodicals are printed on recycled paper that contains at least 50 percent recycled waste, including 10 percent postconsumer waste. Many of our materials are also printed with vegetable-based inks; during the printing process, these inks emit fewer volatile organic compounds (VOCs) than petroleum-based inks. VOCs contribute to the formation of smog.

CONTENTS

EDITOR'S NOTES

The term *enrollment management* has been around for almost twenty-five years. It naturally arose from the recognition that enrollment declines that began in the mid 1970s would not be arrested by better or more recruitment. Rather, colleges and universities would need to integrate a number of activities and programs and, in the process, probably redefine the purposes of many of them. Also, it became clear that an admission office alone, or even one that acted in concert with the financial aid office, should not be solely responsible for maintaining adequate enrollment.

As defined by Don Hossler, probably the leading researcher and writer on the subject, "enrollment management is an organizational concept and a systematic set of activities designed to enable educational institutions to exert more influence over their student enrollments. Organized by strategic planning and supported by institutional research, enrollment management activities concern student college choice, transition to college, student attrition and retention, and student outcomes" (Hossler, Bean, and Associates, 1990, p. 5). Notice that no mention is made of recruitment or admission per se. Also, the emphasis is on exerting influence over enrollment, not controlling or manipulating it.

This volume addresses student affairs professionals, one of the key groups that can exert influence over enrollments, both through their direct actions and through their contact with those who are most responsible for working with prospective students: admission and financial aid professionals. It supplements earlier publications by Jossey-Bass (Hossler, Bean, and Associates, 1990) and others, most of which were written for the staff most directly charged with managing enrollments. Authors in this volume assume that readers are familiar with the subject; we have provided information we felt most important to these colleagues. We have assumed that some of our readers have under their jurisdiction offices of student outreach, admissions, financial aid, or advising and that they want to know more about objectives and activities of such offices.

In Chapter One, I give an overview of enrollment management as it arose from discrete functions in recruitment, admissions, and financial aid to a more elaborate and coordinated plan encompassing many other parts of the institution. Several models are taken from other major sources on the subject.

In Chapter Two, Ann Wright explains how student recruitment is now a marketing function that has become so vital to an institution's health it has taken on a life of its own. Examples of some of the excesses, as well as of good practices, are given.

In Chapter Three, Kathy Kurz describes not only the basic components of financial aid but also the roles of the various partners in the enterprise and, more generally, the financing of higher education.

In Chapter Four, David Borus explores in more detail the broader concept of enrollment management, talking about the need for integration of admissions and financial aid with other campus offices.

In Chapter Five, Shirley Binder and Caroline Aldrich-Langen describe the resources necessary for effective enrollment management. They discuss the cost of managing the two key offices (admissions and financial aid) and describe the personnel needs of modern admissions and financial aid offices.

In Chapter Six, Joann Stedman continues the discussion of necessary resources by addressing the subject of technology. She stresses the usefulness of new technology not primarily as a cost-saver, but as a means of enabling enrollment managers to deploy staff to higher-order functions of service to students, families, staff, and faculty. She emphasizes technology's value in helping to reduce bureaucratic functions so that the institution can focus on the consumer (the student) and the product (education).

In Chapter Seven, I conclude with a review of some of the key issues that will affect enrollments and encourage the reader to not shy away from them.

This volume is not exhaustive on the subject of enrollment management, nor is it a primer for admission and financial aid staff. Some important topics in enrollment management are not covered, and we recommend that readers look elsewhere for analysis. Retention of students is a key feature of good enrollment management, and the literature on it abounds. Discussion of graduate and professional-school enrollments is not covered here. Institutional policy regarding postbaccalaureate education is often radically different from undergraduate education and requires an entirely different treatment. We also do not cover continuing education or postsecondary nontraditional education thoroughly. These types can be key in balancing revenues and contributing to the overall health of an institution and should be treated elsewhere. Community college readers will find much of the book applicable to their settings, but many of the issues in enrollment management important to that sector cannot be covered adequately here. Although admission selection criteria affect enrollment management in many ways, it would be impractical to treat that specific topic here. The variety of factors influencing the choice of such criteria and the relative weight of each is as great as the variety of higher-educational institutions.

That the list of additional topics is sizable underscores a major thesis of this book: enrollment management is a comprehensive concept. It comprises more than a few offices; it is not just a matter of counting students or balancing financial aid budgets. It is dynamic: at different points in an institution's history, some areas that promote good enrollment management will be more important or less important. This fact underscores a second theme: enrollment management staff, as much as any in the institution, need to be aware of their surrounding environment, not just their own workplace. They need to communicate to other campus leaders the significance of external and internal issues in maintaining enrollments and they must be flexible and nimble in their adjustment to circumstances.

I want to express my gratitude to my six colleagues who collaborated with me on this volume. They are among the best in their field and sacrificially carved out time to write about the profession they know so well in order to help colleagues elsewhere.

Rebecca R. Dixon
Editor

Reference

Hossler, D., Bean, J. P., and Associates. *The Strategic Management of College Enrollments.* San Francisco: Jossey-Bass, 1990.

REBECCA R. DIXON is associate provost of university enrollment at Northwestern University.

Enrollment management as a concept is reaching maturity. There are four basic models and many variations.

What Is Enrollment Management?

Rebecca R. Dixon

The term *enrollment management* is a familiar one by now. As a concept, it is reaching maturity. As a practice on many campuses, it takes widely varying forms. There is a certain grandeur, even hauteur, in the term that belies what may be going on. However, in recognition of the challenge to achieve and maintain the desirable mix and quantity of students on a campus in the face of a finite supply of students and financial support, the concept deserves high visibility.

This chapter provides background information on enrollment management, discusses the concept in the context of today's colleges and universities, identifies model types of enrollment management, and outlines an ideal approach to implementing enrollment management principles.

According to Don Hossler, "enrollment management is an organizational concept and a systematic set of activities designed to enable educational institutions to exert more influence over their student enrollments. Organized by strategic planning and supported by institutional research, enrollment management activities concern student college choice, transition to college, student attrition and retention, and student outcomes" (Hossler, Bean, and Associates, 1990, p. 5). Succinctly stated, enrollment management is finding, enrolling, and retaining enough of the kinds of students an institution wants.

Background

In the 1960s, colleges and universities began to experience the effect of the postwar baby boom: there were more eighteen- to twenty-four-year-olds. Affirmative action programs, coupled with a real financial aid system triggered in the late 1950s with the launch of the Soviet *Sputnik,* dramatically increased demand for a college education. Campus facilities and programs expanded.

The extraordinary growth of community colleges in the 1960s underscored the idea that college was accessible to all, perhaps even as a right. Advances in communications and travel made recruitment easier. In the 1970s, computer support simplified mass marketing and analysis of data. Computers made the massive financial aid system possible.

The predictable baby bust that began in the 1970s made it necessary for institutions to decide between deep retrenchment and new programs to attract students. Most opted for the latter, at considerable cost in the shifting of resources. Recruitment was increased. Then, as college costs raced ahead, financial aid was increased. In recent years, the institutional share of financial aid has grown far faster than the federal or state government share, placing considerable strain on many college budgets. Concomitant challenges in other parts of academe magnify the need to stabilize enrollments. The increased access to higher education for nontraditional populations—ethnic minorities, older students, and women—that began in the early sixties was now heightened by the self-serving interests of institutions looking for new sources of students.

The casual observer of college enrollment statistics may be puzzled by the anxiety over or seemingly conflicting data about enrollment counts. In fact, U.S. Department of Education data show more students enrolled in higher education in 1992 than in 1982, for example (*Chronicle of Higher Education Almanac,* 1994). However, there are slight shifts in composition. In 1992, there was a higher percentage of graduate students than ten years earlier; the percentage of students in two-year colleges has also increased since 1982. Individual institutions, feeling enrollment pressures, are less concerned about sheer body count and more concerned about net tuition revenue after all costs are counted, including the higher cost of graduate and professional-school students, financial aid, and handling numerous part-time students in place of fewer full-time students.

As early as the mid 1970s, the term *enrollment management* began to emerge (Maguire, 1976). More sophisticated strategies, as opposed to gimmicky recruitment tactics, were discussed. Kotler's *Applying Marketing Theory to College Admission* appeared in 1976 and was soon followed by others that applied the "crass business term" *marketing* to the hallowed intangible of higher education. There was an emphasis on finding new students, women, minorities, older adults, and part-time students.

Recognition of the importance of preventing attrition grew. As college costs accelerated toward the end of the 1970s, along with a decline in the number of highly qualified applicants, compensating financial aid became more prevalent. Colleges and universities increased their use of merit aid, given as an enticement without regard to financial need. Sharp fluctuations of enrollments and financial aid, as well as eroding student quality, forced institutions to take a more comprehensive approach. No longer was it sufficient to add another recruiter, develop another brochure, or add a little more to the financial aid fund.

Enrollment Management as a Mature Concept

The need to manage enrollments intentionally and closely is now a fundamental policy in postsecondary institutions. The National Association of College and University Business Officers conducted research in 1992 to examine the breadth and depth of financial problems faced by higher education institutions. Findings indicated that university business officers perceived declining enrollment as second only to declining appropriations as the reason for financial problems. On the other hand, a majority of the respondents saw stable or increased enrollment as the number-one reason for institutional stability and strength.

In order to achieve a stable level of the desired enrollment, the goals of enrollment management are as follows:

Define the institution's nature and characteristics, using both objective and subjective techniques, and market it appropriately and aggressively.

Incorporate into marketing plans and activities all relevant campus sectors, making sure that all parties recognize that institutional goals are being served.

Make strategic decisions about the role and amount of financial aid needed to attract and retain students, making certain that this expense serves the institution's goals; in most cases, it can no longer be considered a charitable enterprise.

Make the appropriate commitment of human, monetary, and technological resources.

Enrollment Management Plans

At its best, enrollment management is strategic. It involves comprehensive planning. It is not just a set of recruitment tactics, with financial aid as a main component. A few institutions, enjoying satisfactory enrollments, may not need to establish a new comprehensive scheme. Others may develop an enrollment management plan to obtain more highly qualified students or students of a certain type (such as underrepresented minorities, engineers, or students in the humanities). Public institutions may need a plan that focuses on better distribution of students among its programs, more in-state students, higher retention, or more efficient progress through the four-year program. Private institutions (particularly small liberal arts colleges), with smaller enrollment bases and fewer revenue-producing activities, probably have the greatest need for a strategic enrollment management plan that includes most sectors of the academic community.

Four Models

Don Hossler offers four enrollment management models (Hossler, Bean, and Associates, 1990). Institutions wishing to modify current plans or establish one should look at these:

- The enrollment management committee comprises personnel from across the campus and thereby serves the useful function of informing people of what is needed. However, committees often have little power and only limited influence. A committee might be a good starting point, but a more formal arrangement may be needed.
- Appointing an enrollment management coordinator may not require much formal restructuring and, in contrast to the enrollment management committee, some power is vested formally in an individual. Depending on that person's place in the administrative hierarchy and his or her clout, and depending on the institution's enrollment health, the coordinating approach might suffice. However, the absence of formal links among units can weaken coordination and, therefore, effectiveness.
- The enrollment management matrix is more centralized than the first two because it places a senior administrative officer in charge. It does not require considerable reshuffling of subordinate units, but rather requires that they work together for good enrollment management. A vice president for student affairs, for example, could become the enrollment management head, bringing together reporting units of the offices of admission, financial aid, registrar, student life, residence halls, advising, and so forth. The disadvantages of this arrangement are that the senior officer may not have enough time to concentrate on enrollment management, and the plan still omits other campus units that should be included, such as academic advising, institutional research, and alumni affairs.
- The enrollment management division, as its name suggests, is a major division of the campus and is the most centralized of the four models. It brings together most, if not all, of the elements necessary for strategic planning of enrollment management under one person, who would necessarily have senior rank in the institution and whose sole responsibility is enrollment management. However, it is difficult to restructure a campus in this way in a short period of time. A campus in crisis might need to do so. Others should try to make the transition over several years, possibly at some political and economic expense.

Components of Enrollment Management

The offices or functions of a college or university that would make up an ideal enrollment management scheme include admissions (and if the outreach function is separate from the application-processing function, both offices), registrar's office, financial aid, bursar's (or student accounts) office, orientation, academic advising, campus activities, residence life, minority-specific advising offices, advising offices for nontraditional students, women's support centers, student employment, career planning and placement, learning assistance center, alumni affairs, public relations and publications, institutional research, faculty development and academic planning, and development.

The list is long! All of these functions pertain to enrollment management, although some are found within a single division of the institution. There are few institutions where a broadly comprehensive scheme is actually in place. It is unlikely that some areas, such as faculty development and academic planning, would report to the chief enrollment manager. However, it is important that students' interests, needs, and learning styles and the general expectations of the faculty be considered part of retention planning.

Ideal Enrollment Management

It should be clear that, because of institutional differences, there is no one ideal way of managing enrollments. Rather, in the chapters that follow, the authors elaborate on selected topics of enrollment management by providing factual background for administrators in student services who need to understand the key issues. Collectively, the authors reflect a segment of administration in higher education that has coped with great change and pressure from many constituencies. Because this segment comprises the front-line staff who first meet the prospective beneficiaries of higher education (students and their families), they have recognized the need to be responsive to the marketplace. They and their staffs must continue to be responsive, adapting appropriately and helping to lead the institution to adaptation. Themes of changes to come and glimpses of what the future may require run throughout this volume, and the reader should look for hints and recommendations pertaining to the following points:

More intentionally defining the institution's mission and character so that the necessary choices can be made with respect to programs, office responsibilities, type of staff, training of staff, and other resources

Understanding what prospective students want and what they respond to (not always the same thing)

Maintaining the speed and clarity of response required of the institution

Providing a way to finance educational expenses, probably different from the present means

Being more canny about external partners involved in the educational process (the media, governments, parents, and vendors, for example)

Breaking down stereotypical job classifications and flattening the job hierarchy, at least in enrollment management offices, as a means of distributing work and responsibility more efficiently and effectively

Assessing the costs of doing business and choosing the most productive ones for the institution

Using new technology in the most positive and productive way so as to shift the focus from the process of attracting and retaining students to the service being delivered and to the consumers themselves

Staying abreast of societal and educational changes and factoring in their influence on enrollment management.

References

Hossler, D., Bean, J. P., and Associates. *The Strategic Management of College Enrollments*. San Francisco: Jossey-Bass, 1990.

Kotler, P. "Applying Marketing Theory to College Admission." In *A Role for Marketing in College Admission: Papers Presented at the Colloquium on College Admissions, May 16–18, 1976, at the Abbey on Lake Geneva, Fontana, Wisconsin.* New York: College Entrance Examination Board, 1976.

Maguire, J. "To the Organized Go the Students." *Bridge Magazine,* 1976, 39 (1), 16–20.

U.S. Department of Education. "College Enrollment by Racial and Ethnic Group, Selected Years."*Chronicle of Higher Education Almanac,* Sept. 1994, 41 (1).

REBECCA R. DIXON *is associate provost of university enrollment at Northwestern University.*

*An increase in the college-age cohort in the next fifteen years will bring
a very different ethnic and academic mix of students, thereby creating
new challenges for enrollment managers.*

Admissions Recruitment:
The First Step

B. Ann Wright

Ralph Waldo Emerson observed an unusual recruitment tactic in 1851 as he
visited the newly established University of Rochester: "They had brought an
Omnibus load of professors down . . . and now they had runners on the road
to catch students. One lad came in yesterday; another, this morning. . . . And
they are confident of graduating a class of Ten by the time green peas are ripe"
(Plumstead, Gilman, and Bennett, 1975, p. 519). We have no reason to think
that such tactics were commonplace or that they signaled the beginning of the
aggressive recruitment we see today. Rather, until about 35 years ago, colleges
did little recruiting; they usually just registered students after a brief period of
application-compilation and selection.

Now we recruit (perhaps a better term is *market*) our institutions to
prospective students and their families as a key activity of enrollment management. Recruitment has become so intense that at times it borders on hucksterism. This chapter explains why this practice has arisen and some of its
dangers. It describes some of the major components of recruitment, pointing
out some of the more influential players in the process. Consistent with the
volume's overall theme that enrollment management is here to stay, the chapter concludes by asserting that admissions recruitment will remain and, doubt-
less, expand in the future.

College Marketing

The simplest definition of *marketing* is "to offer for sale." The marketplace is the
place where works, opinions, and ideas are debated or exchanged. With increased
competition, colleges have been forced to expend significant additional resources

New Directions for Student Services, no. 71, Fall 1995 © Jossey-Bass Publishers to go into the public marketplace and convince buyers of the superior value of their product. Bigger numbers result: more prospects on the college's mailing list and, consequently, more travel, postage, publications, phone calls, and the like, to convince those prospects to apply and, ultimately, enroll.

Successful marketing of a college is finding the right fit between student and college and enrolling the right number of students. It is not just spending more money or pursuing recruitment activities frantically. Good marketing results from knowing one's institution, having a full understanding of the image and the perception of the institution, and merging these effectively with marketing publications and activities.

Recruitment Activities

Colleges and universities with robust recruitment programs often divide them into several main categories. There are those aimed at developing prospects, those designed to convert prospects into applicants, and those aimed at turning admitted applicants into enrollees. The success of the institution at each of these stages is often called yield (the percentage of students remaining after moving from one stage to the next).

Not all activities fall neatly into one category. For example, a publication intended to turn a vague prospect into a real applicant might later convert the admitted applicant into an enrolled student. There is much indirect recruitment (summer programs on campus for junior high students or a serendipitous article in a local newspaper, for example), but the list here is confined to activities planned for the purpose of recruitment.

Prospective Stage. Colleges build mailing lists to enable repeated follow-up. Lists are derived from student inquiries by phone, mail, and campus visits, through visits by college staff to high schools, and through other programs where the admission staff or their proxies are present (college night programs, for example). Another major source of names and addresses for prospect mailing lists is from college testing services (The College Board's Student Search Service and the American College Testing's Educational Opportunity Service). There are specialty sources, too, such as those supplying names of Hispanic or African-American youth. Students send test scores to colleges in which they have some interest, providing another source of names.

Colleges write or call these prospects one or more times, often trying to supply information on subjects or characteristics associated with each student. For example, enrolled college students from Florida might call prospects from Florida, or faculty in the history department might call students who have expressed an interest in history. Technology, such as the Internet, is revolutionizing the way colleges communicate with prospective students at all stages of the process.

Colleges with aggressive recruitment programs try to convince prospects to visit the campus and they plan many activities around individual and group visits.

Applicant Stage. When a student submits an application for admission, much more information is available about him or her. This fact enables the college to provide more specific information aimed at the particular characteristics or interests of the applicant. Letters, publications, phone calls, videotapes of the campus or about special programs, and invitations to visit may all be used at this stage, just as they were at the prospective stage, but with greater certainty of the student's interest in the college.

After Admission. Depending on how much time there is between the offer of admission and the nationally accepted student-reply date of May 1, colleges engage in "yield" activities, often intensifying the ones named above. Financial aid awards and other financial information are especially appropriate at this stage because students need to home in on their final decision. On-campus programs in which faculty and staff meet with groups of admittees are useful. At any stage, alumni may plan events for hometown students because students like to meet others who may be attending a college in which they are interested or to which they have been admitted.

Marketing Problems

College recruitment is an enormous enterprise. Even if all of the activity were tasteful and dignified, there is so much of it that students and families are overwhelmed and sometimes dismayed at the cumulative effect. A 1994 paper written by a high school student during the admission year explains her perspective on college marketing: "Colleges must find ways to appeal to people of all ages, races and mindsets in order to survive . . . using various materials to persuade the typical prospective student . . . selling hope, vitality, and prestige. . . . I find it frightening to be manipulated by the various propaganda techniques, but I do not see any way of avoiding them in my college decision-making process—I can only hope that I am really making the right decision" (Simms, 1994, p. 1).

It is little wonder that students react this way after experiencing some of the recruitment tactics of the 1980s and 1990s. Another response is explained in an article appropriately titled "Colleges Overwhelm Most Students with Massive Recruiting Efforts." As the author's daughter begins receiving mail in response to taking the Preliminary Scholastic Assessment Test her junior year, he observes her reaction: "What began as a delighted 'Gee, I wonder if I'll get anything from colleges today?' now has turned into a surly 'I can't believe all this garbage I keep getting from colleges'" (Jorgensen, 1994, p. B3).

Marketing Bordering on Hucksterism. Unfortunately, intense marketing competition may lead to desperation, which may breed hucksterism. A huckster is a hawker or peddler who sells by showmanship. In an attempt to get attention and sell to the family, some colleges have stooped to hucksterism, implementing extreme activities. At a 1994 retreat at Bowdoin College for admission officers and college counselors, a discussion of hucksterism led to a list of feared extremes in the future: colleges hiring trucks to drive through targeted affluent neighborhoods with loudspeakers, exhorting students to apply; selling institutions on "The College Channel," cable television's home shopping network, which would show infomercials at an exorbitant cost to sponsoring colleges; or perhaps the use of television to auction off places in the class.

Absurd as this sounds, many examples of hucksterism have contaminated the admission process: misleading text and photos that the public discovers to be something different (photos of urban skylines for suburban campuses, photos of mountains and lakes hundreds of miles from campuses, and text that suggests world-class experiences in a secondary department or activity) and overly composed photos that misrepresent the institution.

In addition, some colleges purchase names and then call prospects to offer admission at a premium; some simply send offers of admission with scholarships to students before any application. One college released balloons with scholarship certificates inside, to be redeemed by anyone who so chose; others purchase geodemographic name lists and send admission offers and merit awards to high-income students in those areas. A whole new industry of headhunters has been created, with colleges paying them for every student who enrolls (like Emerson's runners on the road).

The conversion of need-based financial aid to large merit awards not based mainly on need in order to enroll certain types of students is another signal of the intensity of the competitive climate. This practice, exercised to an extreme, has stretched some institutional budgets dangerously and, in some cases, with meager offsetting gains on the enrollment side.

Gresham's Law may apply; certain marketing activities may contaminate the process, seeming to drive out the good, so that the public now mistrusts or is skeptical of what is presented to them.

Ethics. Where will the extremes end? One of the best hopes is through professional organizations that establish principles of good practice for their members. The National Association of College Admission Counselors was founded in 1937 for the purpose of establishing a Code of Ethics; more recently, it developed an updated statement of principles with the American Association of Collegiate Registrars and Admission Officers and The College Board. Other education groups have endorsed the statement, which presents ethical admission practices and policies for higher education and secondary school members. The statement covers admission promotion and recruitment, admission procedures, use of standardized college admission testing, financial aid, and the awarding of credit to advanced students. There are monitoring procedures for both member and nonmember institutions, with various possible outcomes, including censure, suspension, and termination of membership. The statement is reviewed annually to be sure it reflects concerns for an environment that changes with technology, new marketing techniques, and legal issues.

There are ongoing concerns in areas such as the honest presentation of information by colleges, the pressuring of students through early deadlines, early decision violations, deposits at more than one college by students, and especially the increased problems surrounding financial aid offers.

Professional organizations can create standards and monitor excessive practice, but colleges must determine the balance between serving their institutions and serving students. College and university officials now recognize that when survival is at stake, institutional demands take priority, inevitably leading to some reinterpretation of accepted ethical practices. In the final analysis, the public will have the last word because extreme activities will be seen for what they are and will force moderation in marketing. Faculty and administrators should be alert to the negative effects of overselling on their own institutions in particular and on higher education in general.

Admission and the Media. As colleges have increased their marketing, so have the purveyors of books, newspapers, and magazines dealing with the college-going process. At one time, college information was disseminated primarily by large tomes filled with brief descriptions and statistics in small print. As the public has become more consumer-oriented, there has been increasing competition among publishing houses, culminating in various ratings and rankings that have affected recruitment practices. College and secondary school counselors deplore this development: "The media had entered the network of relationships involved in the admissions process, displacing counselors and influencing both prospective students and college admissions personnel who must respond to questionnaires on selectivity. Thus the delicate balance among students and family, high school counselor, and college admissions office appeared to be swinging this way and that, moved by the winds of public relations and media hype" (Wright, 1992, p. 6).

These ratings and guidebooks of the "top 100" or "best colleges" are very popular. Why? "The simple answer is that people want lists. Overwhelmed with advertising and clamor, they increasingly turn to the simplicity of the single vertical column . . . in response to our instinct for order and control—the inclination to organize our lives" (Wright, 1992, p. 6).

Much as they might dislike these lists, college admission officers have become very sensitive to the criteria that determine their rankings: SATs, class rank, retention, alumni giving, costs, student/faculty ratios, and so forth. In some cases, outside pressures have forced admission officers to improve their standings on the lists, with stories of admission directors being told to get their institutions on the list at any cost, in some cases leading to manipulation of college statistics. Fortunately, most college representatives recognize that credibility is most important, but the pressure to emphasize the rankings criteria is still there.

College Costs, Financial Aid, and Recruiting. High college costs have forced a greater reliance on financial aid, as colleges use it to meet enrollment targets. However, in order to fund their grant programs, colleges have had to raise tuition and fees, the sources from which most institutions derive most of the money to allocate to grants and scholarships. Trying to conserve financial aid funds, colleges are aggressively recruiting students who do not require financial aid. A major controversy has resulted regarding the equity and even wisdom of recruiting and admitting nonaid students who may be less qualified than financially needy students. These serious policy and ethical issues, along with a consideration of various packaging options and their impact, are discussed in the chapter on financial aid.

Another recruiting solution favored by many colleges is to do everything possible to enroll foreign nonaid students. For a few years, success in this area was a windfall to some colleges, but as the word spread, such recruiting became more competitive. Many admission officers now feel it is almost as difficult to recruit in Asia and Europe as in many parts of the United States. Certainly, it is expensive. At present, one is almost as likely to run into an admission colleague in Seoul or Athens as in Boston or Chicago. A Singapore counselor observed recently that, for successful recruiting, college representatives must visit regularly. Now that the most selective colleges are doing so, the same pecking order of college preference has been established abroad. Wherever these international students enroll, they change both the culture and the demands on student services. Thus, the college needs to plan for the other effects of enrolling foreign students.

The increasing allocation of financial aid funds by colleges has not been sufficient to retain the balance of students from all economic classes, an objective more nearly achieved in the 1960s and 1970s. In particular, high-cost private institutions have seen a large "middle-class melt" in their applicant pools, creating major changes in enrolled populations on campus. Some private institutions fear they are moving toward a bipolar socioeconomic distribution of wealthy students and poor students.

College administrators must be alert to the effects of a shift in the college-attendance possibilities and practices of middle-income students.

Recruitment of Special Categories of Students

Most institutions want to enroll special types of students and justify the diversion of resources (staff and money) to recruit them. Categories include students talented in the performing arts, foreign students, older adults, high-ability students in the sciences or humanities, and so forth. Three categories that are often targeted are underrepresented minorities, athletes, and students whose family members have attended the institution or who are related to known or prospective donors.

Minority Students. In the 1970s, colleges became conscious of the need to take more social responsibility by presenting equal opportunities to all groups of students. Among the many minority groups, those that have received the most attention are Asian-American, Native American, African-American, and Hispanic/Latino (particularly Mexican-Americans and Puerto Ricans). In terms of the percentage who attend college, the underrepresented groups are the last three, all of whom have had lower high school graduation and college-going rates over the years (Western Interstate Commission for Higher Education, 1991).

In an attempt to create a college community that more accurately reflects the population, many admission offices have implemented affirmative action programs that recognize academic potential and the handicaps of a disadvantaged background, thereby giving extra consideration to minority applicants. Some states encourage or require affirmative action plans, which may involve special recruiting, scholarships designed to recruit and retain minority students, and other activities. The constitutionality of minority scholarships was questioned in the early 1990s by the Civil Rights Office of the Department of Education, with another ruling against the scholarships in 1994. It now seems likely that the limited legality of minority-targeted scholarships will continue to be tested in the courts. Although affirmative action causes some political controversy, most admission staffs are comfortable with their abilities to evaluate college potential and select an incoming class with methods that are fair to all students and to the college.

The next decade will bring dramatic changes in the ethnic backgrounds of high school graduates, with so-called minority populations growing at a much faster rate than the white population. For example, although total undergraduate enrollment rose only 3.1 percent between 1990 and 1993, the enrollment of African-Americans rose 12.3 percent in that period and the enrollment of Hispanics rose 26.7 percent (U.S. Department of Education, 1995). As college enrollments change to more accurately reflect the U.S. population, the entire college community must be prepared for the increased demands on student services.

Student Athletes. Like any special talent or ability, athletic potential is regarded as a basis for additional consideration in the admission process. The importance of that characteristic depends on the college and its needs, as well as the ability of the applicant. For an athletic Division I school that hopes to compete nationally, a high-ability athlete will rise to the top of the applicant group; the higher the ability, the better any marginal academic qualifications may appear. For Divisions II and III, those rules may vary depending on institutional priorities. In all divisions, coaches become major players in the recruitment activities, as well as lobbyists for their top candidates. It is desirable to establish and maintain good relations between the admission and athletic offices because the goals may not always coincide. Senior management above the athletic and admission offices should participate in the establishment of athletic recruiting policies and practices to ensure that institutional needs are being served.

Legacies, Development Connections, and Other Special Interests. An applicant may be considered a legacy if he or she has a close relative, or in some cases any relative, who attended the college. Many private institutions exercise flexibility for legacies, sometimes having different policies for the strength of the alumni connection, with parents, grandparents, and siblings usually having the greatest influence. By contrast, public schools are less likely to bend for legacies.

There is a similar policy of flexibility for VIPs, or those singled out by the development offices as having special potential for the college. Again, admission decisions may take into consideration a strong connection or recommendation from a person who is deemed important to the institution. Examples include major donors, trustee recommendations, recognized family names and positions, and others with political pull.

As one might expect, special talents and departmental needs on a given campus receive extra consideration. Some public schools may set a quota for athletic or artistic students or special scholarships that compensate for academic profile weaknesses. In *Playing the Selective College Admissions Game,* Richard Moll mentions the expert oboist, vocalist, or sculptor, as well as the importance given to Bowdoin's annual need for a super hockey goalie who "competes against the two or three other hockey goalies applying. . . . Forget the class rank and the high SATs" (Moll, 1994, p. 119). Also, some "feeder" schools get special attention in order to maintain an important relationship with a school or counselor that has provided a special connection in the past.

Obviously, institutions should handle these special-interest cases with great discretion. Although an admissions quota of such cases is not recommended, a college that is concerned about a growing number of such cases should consider whether the proportion of their new students and the quality of such students is correct and defensible.

Recruiting Beyond Students

Students are heavily influenced by important people in their lives. There may be debate about the rank order of these people (one study indicated that the mother is most important and the family doctor is second), but it appears that peers, family, and school counselors and teachers have the largest influence.

Peers. Depending on the culture of the high school, peers may have an enormous influence because they control the perceived prestige of individual colleges. At many schools, the major discussion among seniors in the fall is "Where did you apply?" and the intense concern of the spring months is "Where did you get in?" In these conversations, colleges can be reduced to labels and students can be sorely tempted to respond to peer pressure rather than making their own decisions.

Parents. As a four-year college education has become a major family investment, parents have become more involved in the selection process. "[S]tudents, mothers, and fathers were all more likely to assign the greatest influence to parents in determining the amount of financial resources that would be available for college" (Litten, 1991, p. 38). Colleges have increasingly aimed their marketing toward parents in order to convince them that a higher education is an investment with value added, that their institutions are affordable, and that the high cost will pay off in the long run in terms of higher incomes, better networking in the workplace, and a more satisfying lifestyle. This kind of recruitment takes various forms: parent brochures, special letters regarding careers and support services, special parental activities for on-campus visits, and staff attention that may include everyone from admission and financial aid staff to the president.

In addition, many parents are now very concerned about campus crime and may request crime statistics and safety information from admission offices. Admission marketers, especially in urban areas, worry about how these statistics might be interpreted. Needless to say, negative statistics are troublesome for all, but particularly frightening for international audiences because parents are highly sensitive to the difficulties and worries of sending their young sons and daughters into a foreign environment.

Guidance Counselors. In former times, secondary school guidance or college counselors were left to their own devices, reading catalogs, visiting colleges on their own, and acting as repositories for the adventurous stories of alumni, to be passed along to prospects. Their knowledge about colleges was based largely on their own initiative, and there was tremendous variation among them in that knowledge. Many counselors did an excellent job; some had more limited horizons. Times have changed, with guidance counselors now perceived by many colleges as major influences in the application process. In some cases they are courted by colleges who sponsor visits to their campuses. Many colleges make special efforts to create personal relationships with guidance counselors, with the result that information may be shared and, in the end, students may be better served as the counselors attempt to make the proper fit.

Independent Counselors. A fairly new phenomenon is the rise of the independent counselor or educational consultant who (for a fee) works with families to select a college, prepare the students for the interview and the application, and write a letter of recommendation. Some are also advising students and families about playing the financial aid game. Independent counselors also do some *pro bono* work with students who are unable to pay a regular fee. In the present buyers' market, the demand for independent counselors has diminished somewhat, with their clients primarily students who are hoping for admission to a competitive college.

However, as the college-bound population rises, the role of both school guidance counselors and independent counselors will again change. Slowly, competition will increase for places in the college class, but counselors will be working with the very different demands and needs of students from more varied ethnic and socioeconomic backgrounds.

Attracting Students: Other Programs and Techniques

Each institution develops recruitment programs that best fit its needs. Some main themes that should be considered are mentioned here.

Early Commitments. For students who make a definite college decision early in the year, colleges have responded with opportunities to make a personal and financial commitment. Rolling admission, offered by colleges that decide as applications arrive, provides students the opportunity to settle early the worry and stress of the application year. Similarly, early action and early decision plans give those students an answer to their applications.

A special example of early action is practiced at California State University, Chico, which hosts a day-long event during which prospective students, completed applications in hand, have their high school transcripts evaluated, and, if qualified, are admitted on the spot. With tears of joy, students and their families immediately pose for pictures with their certificates of admission. At Bard College, applicants may visit the college on selected fall days, attend a two-hour seminar based on reading materials received earlier, and meet with students and faculty. Meanwhile, the admission committee meets to make decisions, and at the end of the day students have an interview and receive the admission decision in person. Such programs are extremely effective in cutting through the bureaucracy of the process and providing instant gratification to the successful candidates, particularly those who are sure of their first-choice college and wish to establish their admission status early in the application year.

Merit Awards, Research Opportunities, and Study Abroad. Increasingly, colleges are attaching special funding and unique opportunities to their offers to the strongest students in their pools. In 1987, The College Board published a study on the effectiveness of merit awards, demonstrating what kind of program would be required to alter college choice. This study showed that if a student were indifferent in choosing between two colleges, it would require $5,000 to move the student from a 50 percent probability to an 81 percent probability of choosing the college offering the additional grant. However, it would actually cost the college considerably more overall because some of the students who were indifferent would have enrolled without merit awards (Chapman and Jackson, 1987). "It is also quite expensive for colleges to attempt to lure a student from a first-choice college through a merit award. In such a case . . . on average, the original first preference colleges would be chosen by the student about 80 percent of the time. Our results predict that the original second-choice college would have to offer an additional scholarship of about $4,700 to improve its chances of choice to 50 percent (from 20 percent)" (Chapman and Jackson, 1987, p. 6).

Just updating Chapman and Jackson's figure to constant dollars, the $4,700 amount today would be about $6,400. That amount is being exceeded by many colleges, both public and private. A recent survey by the National Association of College Admission Counselors indicated that 88 percent of responding colleges are offering some form of merit awards to targeted admittees (National Association of College Admission Counselors, 1994). Beyond simple merit scholarships, offers may include prestigious titles, research opportunities, support for study abroad, large amounts of pocket money, and even money-back guarantees of a job after college.

Consortium Activities. In the past, the admission counselor's travel itinerary included six to eight weeks on the road in the fall, with a visit each day to four high schools and an occasional college night program. The cost of such travel is very high in actual dollars and in staff time, and as students have become increasingly sophisticated about evaluating colleges, the high school visit is now regarded by many as an anachronism. Colleges with major reputations and a very high draw have reduced their high school visitation program and replaced it with a series of large receptions in cities, where both students and parents may attend. Lesser-known institutions find such receptions alone to be inadequate for their recruitment goals.

One solution is for groups of colleges, usually three to eight, to send one delegate each and travel together to a series of locations, often sponsoring evening receptions for students and parents as well as a special meeting for guidance counselors. Families are drawn to programs that allow them to learn about several colleges at one time. Such group activities may also save money for the colleges, but they require significant planning and staff time to provide for purchase of student mailing lists, printing and mailing of invitations and posters, reception arrangements, complex travel for several people, and so forth.

Group activities also include guidance counselor tours to campuses, which may be sponsored by state and regional professional groups as well as institutions. Colleges that can coordinate travel among their campuses may arrange shared counselor visits, with the obvious advantage of shared costs.

In the quest for more efficient and effective recruiting, colleges continue to search for the best activities. The possibility of shared travel, receptions, counselor gatherings, with the ultimate advantage of shared costs, is in tension with the need to be distinctive and to avoid losing prospective students to partners in activities.

Transfers: Recruiting the Second Time Around

With all the talk of recruiting students from high schools, many forget students who wish to transfer from another institution. However, this group is the lifeblood of admissions at some colleges. In fact, in many states, there are detailed articulation agreements between the public community colleges and the public four-year institutions. As two-year transfer students plan their progress toward a degree at a four-year university, these agreements guarantee equivalence in subject matter so that time is not lost in the transfer process; in some cases, they entitle the student to admission and class standing. Students entering senior institutions by this route may have different expectations and needs from younger students who entered straight from high school or with little previous college education. Private four-year institutions eager to attract community college graduates may have similar articulation agreements.

When including community college students, "one College Board official estimates that two out of every five college students will transfer at least once before completing an undergraduate degree" (Dalby and Rubenstone, 1993, p. vii). Transfers often bring maturity and experience, as well as the enthusiasm of the convert who has tried something else and wants to make a better choice. In addition, these students move through the system quickly, sometimes with lower average financial aid. "In the last decade, enrollment grew an average of

17 percent at two-year colleges but only 7 percent at four-year colleges. This means that colleges and universities are more interested than ever in recruiting and enrolling transfers. It also means that the number of students trying to transfer is increasing each year" (Dalby and Rubenstone, 1993, p. 9).

Increasingly, enrollment managers have turned to the transfer pool to help meet recruiting goals. However, at institutions that direct most of their resources toward students who started with them as freshmen, transfers may require different services, both in the recruitment stage and after entrance. Recruiting transfers is different from recruiting freshmen, involving special relationships with community colleges and with nontraditional students, as well as detailed knowledge of a variety of transcript and evaluation processes. The active recruitment of transfers from other four-year colleges is considered bad form, if not an act of war!

Retention: Painless Recruiting

In this day of strategic planning, most colleges are aware of the advantages of a high retention and graduation rate. Taxpayers are pressuring institutions (particularly public institutions) to ensure that students can get the classes they need or want and graduate on time. A proven track record of meeting such expectations is an important component of recruitment.

There are other positive effects of improved retention rates. Obviously, every student who withdraws should be replaced, and this requires resources for recruitment and financial aid. Attrition also may result in a drop in quality if the student who leaves is replaced by a less-qualified student. For example, Smith College, with an entering first-year class of 625, would need to recruit only 610 students if retention were to increase by 2 percent. There would be significant cost and quality savings from recruiting 15 fewer students who are at the margin of the admitted pool. Improved retention results only partially from recruiting at the outset the student who fits the college; even more important is what happens during the four-year academic and social experience.

Future of College Recruiting

Where do we go from here?

The high school graduating numbers are beginning to reverse, with a steadily rising number through the 1990s and beyond. The previous record of 1979 will be exceeded by the year 2008, with a projected total of 3.3 million graduates. Many people think the recruitment pressures will ease with this increase, but in fact there will be very different and very serious challenges to colleges. Far more of this population will be first-generation college students, far more will be immigrants, far more will come from ethnic minority groups, and far more will be socioeconomically and educationally disadvantaged. Most seriously, many of the above groups have significantly lower college participation and completion rates, creating the greatest challenge of all. For example, in 1992 the college-participation rate for all high school graduates was 41.9 percent. For Hispanics, 37.1 percent participated, whereas 33.8 percent of African-Americans were enrolled in college (Carter and Wilson, 1994). These realities suggest the need for radical changes in college preparation, recruitment, and student services for the college students of the future.

College recruitment must adjust to these changes and to the increasingly sophisticated market competition and public expectations we face. Is the future of the campus visit a virtual reality tour? Will admission officers visit schools by satellite teleconference? It is impossible to overstate the potential impact of technology on all recruiting activities, as readers will see in Chapter Six. In addition to new marketing approaches, competition will continue to drive campus offerings, student services, and additional academic programs.

Although it is difficult to describe the recruitment of the future, it is safe to predict that it will continue to be a significant activity of the great majority of institutions. No matter how large the potential supply of students might be—traditional college age or older—colleges will need to work hard to locate the variety they want and to enroll those who best fit their institutions.

References

Carter, D. J., and Wilson, R. *Minorities in Higher Education.* Washington, D.C.: American Council on Education, 1994.

Chapman, R. G., and Jackson, R. *College Choice of Academically Able Students: The Influence of No-Need Financial Aid and Other Factors.* New York: College Entrance Examination Board, 1987.

Dalby, S., and Rubenstone, S. *The Transfer Student's Guide to Changing Colleges.* Englewood Cliffs, N.J.: Prentice Hall, 1993.

Jorgensen, D. "Colleges Overwhelm Most Students with Massive Recruiting Efforts." *Chronicle of Higher Education,* Mar. 23, 1994, p. B3.

Litten, L. H. *Ivy Bound: High-Ability Students and College Choice.* New York: College Board, 1991.

Moll, R. *Playing the Selective College Admissions Game.* New York: Penguin, 1994.

National Association of College Admission Counselors. *Report on the Results of the Membership Survey of Need-Blind and Need-Conscious Admission Practices.* Alexandria, Va.: Sequitur Corporation, 1994.

Plumstead, A. W., Gilman, W. H., and Bennett, R. H. (eds.). *The Journals and Miscellaneous Notebooks of Ralph Waldo Emerson,* vol. 1849–51. Cambridge, Mass.: Belknap Press, 1975.

Simms, L. "Propaganda Techniques in Effect." Unpublished paper for Hawken School, Gates Mills, Ohio, 1994.

U.S. Department of Education, Office of Educational Research and Improvement, National Center for Education Statistics. *Enrollment in Higher Education: Fall 1984 Through Fall 1993.* Washington, D.C.: U.S. Government Printing Office, 1995.

Western Interstate Commission for Higher Education and The College Board. *The Road to College: Educational Progress by Race and Ethnicity.* Boulder, Colo.: Western Interstate Commission for Higher Education, 1991.

Wright, B. A. "A Little Learning Is a Dangerous Thing: A Look at Two Popular College Rankings." *College Board Review,* Spring 1992, 163.

B. ANN WRIGHT is dean of enrollment management at Smith College.

An overview of the changing role of financial aid and financial aid professionals in supporting enrollment and net tuition revenue goals is presented so that these resources can be managed effectively.

The Changing Role of Financial Aid and Enrollment Management

Kathy A. Kurz

The role of financial aid and financial aid professionals is changing from one of supporting a national goal of universal access to higher education to one of supporting institutional enrollment and net tuition revenue goals. Key causes of the change include increased competition for students and the dissolving of the partnership among governments, families, and institutions that had been so effective at making higher education affordable. This chapter explores common institutional strategies for pricing, awarding aid, and controlling the growth of aid budgets in light of this new role and concludes by discussing the new services aid offices must provide to meet their new challenges effectively.

Brief History of Aid

American higher education is unique in the world because, although it began as a system serving society's elite, over time it came to be seen as central to our egalitarian ideals. Today, 66 percent of eighteen- to twenty-four-year-old U.S. high school graduates will attend college, whereas 25 percent or less attend college in most other countries. Financial aid has played a critical role in that transformation. Beginning in the early 1950s, Harvard and Yale began to consider a family's financial circumstances as well as a student's merit when determining who should receive institutional grants. The federal government encouraged this approach in 1958 with the introduction of the National Defense Student Loan program and increased its support in the mid 1960s when it introduced two income-contingent financial aid programs: College Work-Study and the Educational Opportunity Grant. States had been subsidizing state-controlled institutions for one hundred years, but in 1974, they were encouraged to provide income-sensitive assistance to students through the new federal State Student Incentive Grant program. Thus, a partnership was born among students, parents, institutions, and state and federal governments whose purpose was to provide worthy students of any socioeconomic background access to the institutions of their choice.

In the 1960s and early 1970s, most institutions were making financial assistance available in order to attract the best candidates, to draw students from more distant parts of the country, to add racial and ethnic diversity to their classes, and to strengthen specific academic or co-curricular programs. By using financial assistance to make their institutions accessible to talented students from all walks of life, admissions and financial aid professionals were able to construct interesting and diverse entering classes. Early research in the field of financial aid reflected this approach by focusing on how effective aid programs were in improving access to higher education (Leslie and Brinkman, 1988).

In the early 1980s, however, financial aid as Americans had come to know it and the traditional partnership that supported it began to crumble. Today, institutional aid at many of our institutions no longer represents the cost of bringing together an interesting, diverse class. For an increasing number of institutions that have excess capacity, it has become a means of generating revenues by increasing enrollments with no additional fixed instructional costs. In particular, private institutions assess what their prospective students are willing to pay (their price sensitivity) and then offer aid (discount the price) enough to get them to enroll, but no more. The goal is to maximize net tuition revenue (the amount remaining after tuition charges have been offset by institutional financial aid expenses). Even if only a small amount of tuition is generated from each additional student, each new net tuition dollar adds to the bottom line because fixed costs need not increase. As Chester Finn put it, "since colleges . . . do not like to be short of students, since selective price reductions are one way to lure students away from the competition . . . and since it is usually better from the college's standpoint to enroll even a heavily subsidized student than no student at all, institutions of higher education began one-by-one to use student aid as student bait" (Finn, 1984 p. 10).

Often, research in financial aid focuses not on access and choice issues, but on whether individual institutions are spending what they must to meet net tuition revenue goals and not a penny more. William Bowen and David Breneman stress the importance of clarifying whether the role has shifted in a particular institution. "Most educational decision makers naturally want to think of student aid outlays as educational investments, but this tendency can lead to serious errors. For instance, student aid may be capped at an artificially low level because the college doesn't believe it can afford to spend more on student aid—when, in fact, offering some additional aid might add to net revenues by increasing enrollment" (Bowen and Breneman, 1993, p. 14).

The following simple example demonstrates this point. Assume an institution has the capacity to serve 1,000 students. Its current tuition charge is $10,000. With an institutional grant budget capped at $2,000,000, it funds 40 percent of its current student body of 900 (360 students) with an average award of $5,500 from institutional funds. Because of the cap, they denied aid to 100 eligible applicants. None of them enrolled. Normally the yield on need-based aid recipients for this institution is 50 percent. If the cap did not exist and aid had been offered to those applicants, the institution would have seen the following impact on net tuition revenue:

	With Cap	Without Cap
Enrollment	900	950
Gross revenues	$9,000,000	$9,500,000
Aid	$2,000,000	$2,275,000
Net revenues	$7,000,000	$7,275,000

Clearly, this institution would have been better off financially without a cap on its grant budget.

Apart from the enrollment challenges that have put many institutions under capacity, other forces have driven this rapid departure from the traditional role of financial aid in the admissions process.

Dissolving Partnership

The role of institutional financial aid has changed in large part because the roles of the other traditional partners in financing higher education have changed.

Federal Role. Over the last two decades, growth in federal support for students in higher education has flattened, and the emphasis has been more on loans than on grants. Most recently, even grants are seen as something that should be "earned" by students through national service, rather than as an entitlement that supports the societal good produced by participation in higher education. *Mandate for Change,* the Clinton Administration's transition paper on education, clarifies the philosophical basis for the President's National Service legislation: "National service is a civic compact that creates new opportunities for citizens to *help themselves* by helping others" (Kolderie, Lerman, and Moskos, 1992, p. 144; italics added). Higher education has come to be seen by the federal government as an individual good, a means for students to help themselves, rather than a societal good.

As a result, it is highly likely that the emphasis will continue to be on loans or grants for service rather than on aid intended to provide access to higher education. This trend is not specific to any political party. Both Republican and Democratic presidencies have requested reductions in campus-based aid programs (College Work-Study, Supplemental Educational Opportunity Grants, and Federal Perkins Loans) and have concentrated funding increases in the loan area. As a result, from a high in 1975–76 of 79 percent, the percentage of aid awarded as grants has stabilized at about 50 percent in the late 1980s and early 1990s (College Entrance Examination Board, 1993). Pell Grants, on average, now cover less than 10 percent of the cost of the average private college and about 25 percent of the cost of a public college, versus 15 percent and 32 percent, respectively, in the early 1980s (Frances and Morning, 1993). Ironically, as federal support for higher education declines, federal regulation of higher education has increased. Compliance with federal regulations has become more and more burdensome; some recent examples are the new regulations governing accrediting agencies and the attempt to create State Postsecondary Review Entities.

However, all indications are that the federal funding emphasis will be on elementary and secondary education for the foreseeable future. Universal higher education is no longer a federal goal, and the existing differences in college-going rates by family income (with students from families of incomes over $75,000 being three times more likely to enroll in college than students from families of incomes under $15,000) will persist (Frances and Morning, 1993) and perhaps even grow.

State Role. The state's role in the partnership has seen similar deterioration. Most states face unprecedented budget strains, given the increasing costs of supporting prisons, Medicaid, and other social programs, combined with declining tax revenues produced by a weak economy. Public higher education institutions' share of state government expenditures has declined from a high of over 23 percent in 1968 to a low in 1992 of 17.3 percent (*Postsecondary Education Opportunity,* 1994). In *Keeping College Affordable* (1991), McPherson and Schapiro conclude that "without significant changes in the financing system, it is the population of lower-income students whose educational opportunities would be most severely threatened" by the declining ability of states to finance high-quality education while keeping tuitions low (p. 214). They propose "a change in federal policy [that] would provide states with a powerful incentive to raise their tuitions to cover a much more substantial percentage of their costs" (p. 196). Even without the proposed changes in federal policy, several states are reducing their across-the-board subsidization of families and moving to a high-tuition, high-aid approach.

Under this approach, additional revenues from students and families, obtained through higher tuition charges, make up for reduced taxpayer support. This approach is particularly feasible given that in 1990, 75 percent of the students aged 18–24 from families with incomes over $50,000 were enrolled in public institutions (Frances and Morning, 1993). Clearly, a very large proportion of higher income students are taking advantage of state-supported tuitions, resulting in the "middle-income melt" from private institutions noted in Chapter Two. Interestingly, in New York State, the average income of families receiving need-based state financial aid is lower for recipients attending private institutions in the state than for recipients attending public institutions (Commission on Independent Colleges and Universities, 1992). Clearly, at least in New York State, institutional aid programs play an even more important role than low state tuition levels in assisting low-income students.

Because many states increased state tuitions in the early 1990s, public institutions as a group increased tuition at annual rates exceeding 10 percent, whereas private institutions, reacting to public concern over the rate of tuition increases in the 1980s, slowed their rate of growth to about 7 percent (College Entrance Examination Board, 1993). Unfortunately, in many states the new revenues generated by higher state tuition charges were not available to enhance state-funded need-based aid programs, thus jeopardizing low-income families' access to public higher education. In fact, support for state-funded financial aid programs has declined in many states. For example, in 1991–92, New York reduced the maximum need-based grant under its Tuition Assistance Program, historically one of the most generous need-based state programs in the country, at the same time that state school tuitions increased for the second year in a row after six years of no increases (Regents Commission on Higher Education, 1993).

Other states are simply reducing appropriations to state institutions. *The Chronicle of Higher Education* reported in 1992 that public colleges and universities in 17 states had received state appropriations below 1990 levels (Jaschik, 1992). Some states are also reducing or eliminating long-standing subsidies to private institutions. Unlike the high-tuition, high-aid strategy (which, if implemented correctly, could strengthen the partnership among families, institutions, and states), these other approaches further crumble the partnership and create a situation in which no one wins.

Institutions lose because they no longer have the resources to support a high-quality academic program. Students lose for two reasons. First, the quality of their education is jeopardized. Second, students of less advantaged backgrounds are often excluded from higher education because the heavily subsidized state institution seats are taken by more affluent students with stronger academic backgrounds, and private institutions cannot afford to provide enough financial assistance. The state itself loses because industries will not be attracted to a state with a weak educational system.

Role of Families. The role of students and parents in the partnership is also changing. Families have developed a sense of entitlement and keen negotiating skills. As one college president puts it, "We have learned to tuck away some financial aid leverage for the annual negotiations of the spring" (Moll, 1994, p. 13). Parents' willingness to sacrifice to send their children to college is evaporating as they face a more and more uncertain economy, as the benefits of choosing one institution over another seem less clear and quantifiable, and as colleges seem more and more willing to bid for their children. Students and parents are seeking a clear return on their investment and colleges and universities must respond with factual evidence of the value of the outcomes they produce.

Families—particularly middle- and upper-income families—who have seen rapidly growing cost differences between private and public institutions question whether the value added by attending a private college is worth the price difference. In many cases, they put limits on their willingness to pay, despite the financial aid office's calculation of their ability to pay for college. One way this limit-setting is played out is through increasing demand for heavily subsidized public institutions. Another way is through intergenerational transfer of responsibility for paying for college. With the expansion of eligibility for federal student loans resulting from the Reauthorization of the Higher Education Act in 1992, one sees students borrowing more and more, in many cases to cover what would have been a parental contribution in prior years. For example, under the Federal Stafford Loan Program, independent students can now borrow, under a combination of subsidized and unsubsidized loans, a cumulative maximum of $46,000 for undergraduate studies and a cumulative maximum of $138,500 for undergraduate and graduate studies combined. Before the Reauthorization, these borrowing limits were far lower: $37,250 in Stafford and Supplemental Loans for Students for independent undergraduates and $74,750 for undergraduate and graduate studies combined.

Role of Institutions. Institutions, trying to achieve desired enrollment outcomes in the face of this crumbling partnership, have committed an increasingly larger proportion of their tuition income to financial aid. In 1992–93, institutions committed approximately $7 billion to aid for students, an increase of 75 percent in current dollars over the five years since 1988–89. During that same period, funds for the federal Pell grant program increased by 38 percent in current dollars (College Entrance Examination Board, 1993). It is not uncommon for the "discount rate" (financial aid as a percentage of gross tuition revenues) at many private institutions to be as high as 30 to 40 percent, up from half that rate ten years ago.

At the same time, however, institutional awarding strategies have become increasingly targeted. Aid awards can range from full merit scholarships (based on qualifications other than need) for students most in demand to large unmet need and high loan and work expectations for students with fewer attractive qualities. Thus, although institutions still play a critical role in the financing of higher education through their pricing and discounting strategies, their role in the partnership has changed. In the past, particularly at public institutions with low costs and limited discretionary aid, financial aid officers could focus on issues of access and equity. Now they must identify which populations could or should be targeted for aid, given their price sensitivity as determined by their need and their attractiveness to the institution (Dowling and Scannell, 1993).

Financial Aid Strategies

Before discussing specific financial aid awarding strategies, it is important to recognize that they go hand in hand with pricing strategies. During the 1980s, many institutions raised their tuition charges two to three times the rate of inflation. These increases were necessary for a variety of reasons. Some institutions were compensating for having fallen behind in faculty compensation during the 1970s. Others were responding to changes in the earnings of their endowment portfolio or challenges to other income streams that were not able to keep pace with growth in expenditures. An almost universal factor driving such increases was the tapering off of federal and state financial aid and a concomitant need to increase institutional financial aid. However, this high-tuition, high-aid strategy was not the only option. Some institutions, such as Washington and Lee, deliberately kept tuition increases modest and severely limited the growth of their financial aid programs. Other institutions, such as Duke, felt that they were underpriced for the market, and increased their tuition without rapidly increasing their financial aid. More recently, institutions such as Drake and Worcester Polytechnic Institute have announced tuition freezes, and others have even considered across-the-board reductions in tuition in the hopes of bettering their enrollment picture.

The decision to follow a particular pricing strategy, or to follow any given financial aid awarding strategy, must be driven by a clear understanding of the institution's market position. There is no single right answer to the pricing/financial aid conundrum. Rather, the answer must emerge from an understanding of the institution's competition, trends in students applying for aid, yield rates for students of different quality and need levels, and the institution's perceived value in the marketplace. Admissions and financial aid offices must be able to demonstrate that they are worth the price they are charging. An excellent primer on such analysis is *The Effect of Financial Aid Policies on Admission and Enrollment* (Scannell, 1992).

Merit Versus Need-Based Awarding. In reviewing current strategies used to award financial aid, the distinction that typically comes to mind first is need-based aid versus merit awards. Merit awards are offered without regard to the financial circumstances of the family, whereas need-based aid is offered based on a determination of the family's ability to meet college expenses. The decision to offer merit awards is often a controversial one, as it is seen on many campuses as directly reducing the resources available to meet the need of needier applicants who may be less in demand. However, the changes in the federal formula for determining need that occurred with the 1992 Reauthorization of the Higher Education Act have resulted in a blurring of the distinctions between need-based and merit aid and have undermined the approach to determining family ability to pay that had been used by institutions across the country for years.

Before the 1992 Reauthorization, need was determined by subtracting from the institution's estimated cost of attendance (including tuition and fees, room and board, personal expenses, books, and transportation) a contribution from the student and his or her parents. This family contribution was determined by a universally used formula that considered thirty-five different variables that affect a family's ability to pay for college. The variables included parental income, taxes, the number of people in the family, the number of students in college, and the assets of the parent and student. Because this formula was used by most institutions in the country, a family's contribution would vary little from school to school, and their need would vary only as a result of differences in charges among colleges. That need would then be met as fully as possible with a combination of loans, work awards, and grants or scholarships from the remaining partners in the financing of higher education, generally the federal and state governments and the institution.

With the 1992 amendments to the Higher Education Act, a new federal methodology was established for determining a family's ability to pay for college. It expanded the definition of *need* primarily by eliminating home and farm equity from consideration in determining the family's resources. Under the new formula, the typical middle-class family shows $2,000 to $3,000 more need than they would have under the old approach. At the University of Rochester, meeting that higher level of need for all students would have cost the institution approximately $9 million in 1993–94. Because no additional federal grant funds were allocated to meet that higher level of need, however, and because the strain on institutional aid budgets prohibited universal acceptance of the new definition, means of determining need now vary dramatically from institution to institution and, within some institutions, from student to student, depending on the attractiveness of the applicant. Essentially, this change has created an environment where institutions can bid for the best and the brightest, even where need-based federal aid is involved, as long as they stay within the very loose federal definition of need. The result is fewer resources available to the least advantaged students. A particularly striking example of the current lack of uniformity in awards that are "need"–based is one documented by *U.S. News and World Report* in which a student received an award from one institution under which her family would have to pay only $8,000 of the $26,000 budget, whereas another equally priced institution had determined her to be ineligible for need-based aid (Sanoff, 1993).

For several years, this price competition has occurred outside the need-based arena, with a growing number of institutions offering aid to nonneedy students through a variety of merit-based scholarship programs and discounting schemes. This practice has been most common among institutions using aid to generate net tuition revenues. In fact, until recently, some of the most expensive, most highly selective institutions in the country formally agreed to use their funds only for need-based aid in order to focus their aid program on the original purpose of financial aid: providing access for students of all socioeconomic levels. The Justice Department questioned this practice, and now a settlement has been reached that allows institutions to make such an agreement, but only if the institutions also agree to admit students without regard to need and to meet fully the need of every admitted student. Because so few institutions can meet these conditions, it is probable that even the most prestigious institutions in the country will eventually offer merit awards to ensure the quality of their enrolling class. As a recent *Washington Post* editorial put it, "The idea of keeping aid spread widely by calculating it according to a common formula no longer functions even as an ideal" ("Tuition Trap," 1994, p. A22).

Financial Aid Packaging. Even using the pre-1992 definition of need, there are many approaches to packaging aid (putting together the proportions of grant versus loan and work, or self-help, in an award to a student). Because grant funds are more attractive to students than funds they must borrow or earn, the relative proportions of these types of aid in the package can be as important as the aid total in determining where a student will enroll. These approaches reflect different philosophies and strategies and, predictably, have different effects on net tuition revenue.

Uniform Self-Help or "Equity" Packaging. This strategy calls for the same level of self-help to be awarded to each student, regardless of the relative level of need or the merit of the student. For example, if an institution sets its standard self-help level at $2,500, each student is eligible for loans and work-study amounting to $2,500, whether his or her need is $5,000 or $10,000. The lower-need student would then receive grants of $2,500 and the higher-need student would receive grants of $7,500. Because of its inherent consistency and fairness, this strategy is attractive if the need levels of the students and the resources of the institution allow the standard loan and work levels in the package to be competitive in the marketplace. This approach is most common in public institutions and in prestigious private institutions that use financial aid to shape, rather than to fill, the class.

Differential Self-Help Based on Need. In this approach, loan and work levels vary based on the need level of the student. Often under this strategy, self-help is a fixed percentage of need. For example, an institution may set self-help at 25 percent of need, so a student who needs $5,000 will receive loans and work-study of $1,250, whereas a student who needs $10,000 will receive loans and work-study of $2,500. This approach tends to offer the most attractive packages to the students with the lowest need, regardless of the merit of the student. Some institutions exaggerate this effect by packaging grant aid first to a set level (for example, $5,000) before offering any self-help. In other institutions, self-help may be capped at some level determined to be the maximum students are willing or able to borrow and work.

Differential Self-Help Based on Attractiveness. In this approach, the institution awards lower levels of loan and work-study to the students who are considered the most desirable in their applicant pool. The desired attributes could vary from institution to institution. Racial/ethnic heritage, academic ability, musical or artistic ability, geographic origin, a particular major, and demonstrated leadership might cause a student to be awarded preferentially. Under this strategy, an institution would set various levels of self-help expectations, such as $2,000 for top recruits, $4,000 for average recruits, and $6,000 for the least attractive students in the applicant pool. This approach is typically used by institutions that hope to increase enrollment of the most desired students in their pool by offering attractive aid awards. They then balance their budget by offering less attractive awards to students who typically enroll at a higher rate and for whom the competition is less fierce.

Merit Within Need. This approach combines the last two, varying loan and work levels by both the need of the student and by his or her attractiveness in the pool. For example, an institution might build financial aid packages using three different ratios of self-help to need: 15 percent for very attractive students, 25 percent for average students, and 40 percent for the least attractive students. With these ratios, three students, each with $10,000 of need, could have very different awards, one with self-help of only $1,500, another with $2,500, and the third with $4,000. Like the other approaches described, this one must be driven by a factual understanding of the price sensitivity of various subpopulations in the applicant pool and an understanding of the enrollment goals of the institution.

Negotiation. More and more institutions are revising financial aid awards after the original offer is extended in order to enroll the student. Some of this negotiation always took place, typically in response to more detailed information about a family's financial circumstances. Financial aid officers have always used their professional judgment to alter the standard formula to respond to unusual individual circumstances. For example, families might inform the aid office of an expected decline in their income or of financial obligations not reflected on the standard aid application. In response, aid officers, wanting to ensure the student's ability to enroll, would adjust the original aid award.

Today, however, negotiation has become an important part of the recruiting process. In the spring of 1994, Carnegie Mellon University sent hundreds of aid recipients a form on which they could request a review of their financial aid package. The form stated, "Carnegie Mellon wants to be competitive with your other college choices. . . . If you've received a financial aid package from us that is not competitive with other offers, please let us know" (Carnegie Mellon University, 1994). Institutions are more and more often making exceptions to their own policies on need analysis, packaging, or merit awards in order to match the offers of other schools. Clearly, negotiation and matching strategies must be understood and evaluated like any other awarding strategy in order to ensure that the institution is spending financial aid dollars wisely.

Awarding Upperclass Students. Often, policies for upperclass students are forgotten in the struggle to get the new class. Obviously, however, if financial aid policies for upperclass students do not support the retention of students, overall enrollment goals will suffer. Institutions take a variety of approaches to renewing aid awards. Some commit to a constant level of self-help throughout the student's four years. Others commit only to the original grant, provided need levels do not change dramatically. Still others increase self-help levels for upperclass students at a set rate each year. Whatever the strategy, research on those who leave is essential to assess whether upperclass aid policies are detrimentally affecting retention.

Search for Price Sensitivity. These strategies may indicate that need analysis is a thing of the past and that the future lies in price sensitivity analysis. Clearly, the family's financial circumstances are a major factor in price sensitivity, as is the quality of the student. However, a number of other factors could well be important in determining a family's willingness to pay for a particular institution. Distance between the student's home and the institution, where the institution falls on the student's preference list, the aid-packaging policies of the other schools to which the student has applied, and the academic program of interest to the student are only a few examples of factors that could become part of a sophisticated assessment of the student's likely response to a particular aid offer. If such formulas became common, pure need analysis could well be outdated.

Cost of Need-Blind Admission and Meeting Full Need

Many institutions, after seeing the rapid increase in their financial aid budgets, are seeking means to slow that growth rate. The targeted awarding practices described earlier are one means of distributing limited dollars effectively. At many institutions, however, targeted awarding strategies themselves are not sufficient to limit the aid expenditures as much as is desired. Consequently, these institutions are reexamining their long-standing policies of admitting every qualified student regardless of need (commonly called need-blind admission) and committing to meet the full need of every admitted student. Such reexamination is the source of great furor in the financial aid, admissions, and high school guidance communities. Article IV.A.9 of the Statement of Principles of Good Practice espoused by members of the National Association of College Admission Counselors (1994) states that members will "not use financial need as a consideration in selecting students" (p. 27). In September 1994, the membership discussed whether this standard should be reviewed and how it should be enforced. Although the statement was not changed, no sanctions will be imposed on schools that do not follow it. Recently, a group of counselors from private high schools in New York City distributed a letter nationwide to college and university presidents in which they threatened to dissuade their students from attending institutions that deny admission to some students solely because the institution cannot meet their need.

Despite the controversy that surrounds these issues, institutions are asking themselves whether they can afford to support their current number of needy students without jeopardizing other important aspects of their educational mission. Many colleges, including Smith, Bowdoin, Carleton, and Oberlin, as well as universities such as Brown and Washington, have recently announced they will no longer guarantee to admit entirely on a need-blind basis. Many other institutions are making those same decisions quietly as they admit (or do not admit) students from their waiting list. Many more institutions are admitting students but denying them financial assistance from the institution. Others are "gapping" students, offering a financial aid award that does not fully meet their demonstrated need.

Institutions, like federal and state governments, are reaching the limits of their ability and willingness to support egalitarian ideals. Their focus is on survival, and aid office strategies have changed to reflect that new focus.

Financial Aid Office Services

As the role of the aid office in enrollment management has shifted from providing access and shaping the class to supporting net tuition revenue expectations and filling the class, the services provided by the office have also changed.

Services are being developed for families who previously would have had no contact with the office. Many aid offices now have names such as Office of Student Financial Services, Financial Advisement Center, and the like to reflect their new focuses. Of course, the traditional services must be offered to the growing number of need-based aid recipients.

Traditional Services. Traditionally, the aid office has focused on processing applications for financial aid from students requesting need-based assistance. They keep track of application materials, clarify and verify the information provided, determine and communicate an aid award, process the paperwork for loans, handle grants and scholarships made to students from sources outside the institution, and monitor compliance with federal and state regulations regarding aid programs. The specific services to students and parents that are a part of this traditional role are communicating affordability, counseling, and processing services.

Communicating Affordability. Tremendous misconceptions exist regarding the cost of college and the availability of financial aid. In part, those misconceptions are the result of the complexity of the mix of aid programs available and the dramatic changes in eligibility for federal aid programs that have occurred over the life of those programs. In part, they are a reflection of media attention to the most expensive schools in the country and the reality of sticker prices that can vary by more than $10,000 for one year of college. Finally, in part they are the result of an incorrect assumption on the part of most families that only very poor families qualify for assistance.

Regardless of the source of the misconception, one critical service of the aid office must be to break down those misconceptions and help families understand that a college education is affordable. Most aid offices have a brochure explaining the various sources of aid and demonstrating the range of family incomes that can qualify for those aid programs. In addition, aid officers typically reach out to the community, presenting at local high schools, speaking on radio shows, manning financial aid hotlines, traveling with admissions officers, and in other ways spreading the word about the availability of financial aid.

Particularly at private institutions, these services are critical to the institution's ability to develop an applicant pool. The institution should periodically evaluate the effectiveness of its strategies for communicating affordability to ensure that they are not missing applicants who falsely assumed the institution's price was beyond their reach. One means of determining whether a high-priced institution is effectively communicating affordability is to examine the set of institutions with which the institution overlaps when SAT or ACT scores are first sent versus the set of institutions with which the institution's applications overlap. If the former set includes institutions with wide variability in their charges, but the latter set includes only equally high-priced institutions, it is clear that for some students early interest in the institution may have been dashed because students thought they could not afford it. Public institutions can make a similar assessment by examining how the financial profile of their families compares with those of other families in the state. Does it indicate the loss of students from certain income bands who may have concluded they could not afford college?

Counseling. This service may well be underrated by those outside the aid office who think of the aid process as mechanistic and driven by formulas. As was mentioned earlier, the role of professional judgment in adjusting the formulas by which need is calculated to reflect the true circumstances of the student is critical to attracting and retaining students. Much of the counseling that takes place in an aid office is designed to help the aid officer understand and address those special circumstances. Even when special circumstances are not the issue, families need to feel heard, they need advice on meeting their share of the costs, and they need help in understanding their options and responsibilities. Financial issues are often the surface problem hiding deeper and more painful issues. However, most financial aid officers do not have a counseling background. Training in listening skills, communication skills, and customer service expectations is just as important as training in the details of federal and state regulations and formulas to ensure effective delivery of counseling services. Typically, the former are omitted, and institutions and staff, as well as students and parents, have paid the price.

Processing. The system for receiving and evaluating aid applications and notifying students of their awards must be impeccable and efficient. The timing and accuracy of aid awards is absolutely critical to enrolling and retaining students. Many institutions now try to include aid offers with the offer of admission to seal the deal with the student. Errors in assessing need can cause an institution to lose a student to an institution that presented a more accurate offer. Given the volume of papers, the complexity of the various formulas for determining need and awarding financial aid, and the volatility of federal and state regulations, computer system support for the aid office is critical to effective processing services. For more detailed discussion of these technological needs, see Chapter Six.

Nontraditional Services. The best aid offices are now offering a variety of new services to all students and families, regardless of financial need.

Institutional Work Programs. The traditional college work-study program was intended to provide needy students with another source of financial support. More and more, however, all students are interested in working, and they are looking for positions that are career related and educationally purposeful as well as financially beneficial. Programs such as Reach for Rochester, the Cornell Tradition, and the series of programs sponsored by Dana Student Aid for Educational Quality grants develop internship-like work opportunities for students to help them explore different career fields, build connections between their academic interests and the "real" world, and improve their chances of competing for full-time work after graduation. Although these programs are not always housed in the financial aid office, coordination with that office is critical, and financial aid officers and admissions officers must be able to talk effectively about the programs to prospective students and parents.

Institutional Loan Programs. With the expansion of the federal parent loan program in 1992, under which any family may borrow an amount equal to the full cost of education minus any financial aid they are receiving, the need for institutionally based family loan programs has diminished. Nevertheless, many institutions continue to offer loans with attractive interest rates, repayment terms, or insurance options in an effort to increase the enrollment of full-pay families. In some cases, these loans are actually funded institutionally, often as an investment of endowment resources. In other cases, institutions may gain access to private or state loan funds for families by guaranteeing the loans or by setting up escrow accounts for bad debt. Finally, some institutions merely put an institutional wrapper on a set of private loan programs that they want to present as options to students' families.

Payment Plans. Most institutions now offer a variety of payment plans, including such options as a discount or a guaranteed tuition rate for paying up-front for a year or for all four years, paying the annual charge over an eight- to twelve-month period without interest, paying in two installments, and paying with a credit card. In some cases, these plans are administered locally. Other institutions accept externally administered plans.

Savings Plans. Some institutions are now speaking with the families of young children regarding saving for college. In the mid 1980s, understanding the public concern that tuitions were rising so rapidly as to not be affordable in ten years, many institutions considered offering guaranteed tuition prepay-ment plans or tuition savings plans to parents of potential future enrollees. The states of Michigan and Florida offered such plans to state residents wishing to prepay tuition for their younger children. Even the federal government got into the act with the introduction of tax benefits for savings bonds used to pay tuition. Most of the guaranteed tuition prepayment plans have proven finan-cially infeasible or have tax implications that make them unattractive as an investment vehicle. (The U.S. Court of Appeals for the Sixth Circuit ruled in November of 1994 that the Michigan program is not subject to federal income taxes, so a resurgence in such programs may result.)

The savings plans have not significantly increased the abysmally low rate of saving for college. In general, Americans save at a rate below that of any other economically developed country. "Japan, for example, with half our pop-ulation saves three times as much" ("College Savings and Prepayment Plans," 1988, p. 12). Nevertheless, many aid officers find the power of saving so com-pelling they continue to search for forums in which to educate families about savings vehicles, the minimal impact of saving on financial aid eligibility, and the difference saving can make to a family's monthly college payment. In fact, College Scholarship Service's committee on needs analysis proposed a way of calculating family contributions, called SAFE (Sustained Annual Family Effort), that calculates necessary savings based on the family's historical income stream, and many aid officers have incorporated this concept into their conversations with families about their expected contributions.

Scholarship Search Services. Until recently, most financial aid offices kept on a dusty back shelf a handful of reference books in which students could search for private scholarship and grant programs. They also advised students against using private scholarship search firms, which typically "guaranteed" that they would find five sources of aid for a $40–$75 fee. These services almost always used out-of-date databases, named sources that had restrictions that eliminated most applicants, or supplied information about standard federal and state aid programs that the student could have gotten for free from the aid office. With the advent of the College Scholarship Service's scholarship search software program ("College Cost Explorer Fund Finder"), introduced in 1993, many colleges are now beginning to make scholarship search services a standard part of their program offerings. They hope that such a service will assist upperclass students in meeting tuition increases or in lowering the amount they need to borrow or earn during the academic year.

Financial Advising. Some institutions are now training or hiring staff to provide financial advice to families that do not qualify for financial aid, yet still need financial services. Such advice often resembles that offered by independent financial consultants or private banking services, including the tax implications of different options for liquidating assets to meet college expenses, the pros and cons of different family loan alternatives, and options for reducing a student's costs. Like the other services described above, this new role for financial aid officers is emerging in response to the growing concern about net tuition revenue and the consequent interest in making the institution attractive to families that do not demonstrate financial need.

Encouraging the Institution to Consider Programs that Enhance Affordability. At some institutions, financial aid offices are now becoming advocates for institutional programs and policies that make the institution more affordable to all students. Shortening the time to degree, offering five-year combined bachelor's and master's degree programs, and creating cooperative education programs that offer substantial financial compensation are examples of such programs that are more commonly being implemented.

Role of the Aid Officer

As the role of the aid office has changed, so has the role of the financial aid officer. Aid officers have always had to balance the competing demands of multiple masters: students and parents, sponsoring agencies (including federal and state governments), and the institutions. They have always had to be good counselors and stewards of funds. But now aid professionals are institutions' pricing experts in an increasingly cutthroat marketplace. They must manage and explain an increasingly complex environment, often with reduced staff resources. As they take on these new roles, aid officers should adopt a total quality approach to management, incorporating attention to their customers, effective teamwork, management by fact, planning, and continuous process improvement.

Attention to Customers. Financial aid officers must be aware of the needs of prospective and enrolled students and their families and strive to meet those needs. Additionally, aid offices must establish a means of constantly tracking and understanding the ways in which they are meeting or failing to meet their customers' expectations. Measuring the quality of service delivery is much more difficult than measuring the quality of a product. Most often, the service is performed in a private counseling session, on the telephone, or over the front desk. It is fleeting and difficult to standardize, but financial aid officers cannot let that difficulty stand in the way of their measuring the quality of their services. Methods such as tracking the volume and reasons for telephone calls, asking students to complete a survey immediately after an appointment, monitoring complaints, calling the office periodically to see how long the delays are, interviewing graduating seniors, and conducting focus groups with subsets of customers are all possible means of measuring how well the office is meeting customer expectations. Without such analysis, even offices that currently are providing the desired services in the desired manner will fail to keep pace with the changing expectations of students and their parents.

Effective Teamwork. Financial aid officers today must be equal partners with their admissions colleagues in enrollment management. Admissions and financial aid systems must be linked to ensure the smooth transition of students between offices. Moreover, officers must be aware of each other's policies to ensure that they are not counterproductive. A common example of a counterproductive policy is when an aid office offers financial assistance to continuing students who were originally admitted with no aid (because they were of lower ability) and thus limits the office's ability to fund new students of higher ability. This subject is covered more fully in Chapter Four.

Management by Fact. Financial aid directors must be data analysts in their search for price sensitivity to ensure they spend enough, but not a penny more, and that the institution's sticker price is set with the market in mind. They should analyze changes in yield (the percentage of admittees who enroll) over time for different subgroups of applicants, conducting breakeven analyses of possible new targeting strategies, and testing the market through carefully conducted experiments with pricing strategies.

Planning. Aid officers must be planners, modeling the future implications of today's strategies and decisions. Their models must be simple, yet flexible. Effective models must consider the key variables affecting enrollment, retention, and financial aid costs, yet not be so detailed that no one can understand or believe the results. The models must be based on historical trends, yet be capable of reflecting the effect of strategies designed to change those trends.

Continuous Process Improvement. Aid officers must be sophisticated managers of processes and financial and technological resources. Financial aid processes, perhaps more than almost any others on a university campus, lend themselves to computerization, process flow diagramming, and, consequently, improvement. With constantly changing federal and state regulations, it is easy to have new steps layered onto old processes without ever taking the time to step back and say, "Why are we doing it this way?" or "Why are we doing this at all?" With attention constantly on the customer, knowing which processes are most critical to delivering services that meet their expectations, the aid officer must empower everyone in the office to look at existing procedures with a critical eye.

Other Roles. In addition to being effective quality managers, financial aid officers have other, more public roles. They must be political activists, working toward the continued support of the federal and state partners in a time of increasing fiscal challenge. With the traditional partners in financing higher education reducing their roles, financial aid officers must seek out new partners. They must be fundraisers, in concert with their development offices, capable of making the case for funds to major donors or corporations and foundations. Finally, they must be educators of the institutional leadership regarding aid and pricing issues.

Much of what has been discussed in this chapter is not widely understood outside the financial aid office. As a result, policies can be set without the policy makers understanding the implications of their decision. An example of this educating role occurred recently in a private secondary school, but the scenario probably has been played in higher education settings. The board of this school had set the growth in the aid budget at one percentage point above the annual increase in tuition. They thought they were increasing the aid budget, proportionately, more than they were increasing tuition. By doing so, they believed they would make themselves more accessible to needy students. The following arithmetic—straightforward, yet for many counterintuitive—convinced them otherwise:

$20,000 tuition, room, and board x 6 percent = $1,200 increase in charges
$900,000 aid budget x 7 percent = $63,000 more aid
$63,000 ÷ 60 current aid recipients = only $1,050 increase in aid per student to cover $1,200 increase in charges.

Therefore, either aid recipients will be gapped by $150 each or additional aid will have to go to meet the gap, leaving $9,000 less for new students, rather than leaving more to help boost access for needy students.

Once convinced, this board moved forward with a more realistic view of what their policies could and could not be expected to produce.

This last role as educator will determine the aid officer's ability to inform policy and resource decisions that will ultimately determine the chances for success in meeting the institution's enrollment challenges.

Significant Change Is Forecast

We have discussed the changes that have occurred in the purposes of aid programs and in the partners who support them. We have described the leadership and analytical, technical, and planning skills necessary to manage financial aid programs effectively in this new world. However, the enormous changes that have occurred mark only the beginning. They will be followed by further change as government support continues to decline, as funding shifts among sectors and among aid programs, as old standards and agreements further disintegrate, and as new partnerships are sought.

References

Bowen, W., and Breneman, D. "Student Aid: Price Discount or Educational Investment?" *Trusteeship,* May/June 1993, pp. 11–15.

Carnegie Mellon University. "Request a Review of Your Financial Aid Package." Form used by the financial aid office, 1994.

College Entrance Examination Board. *Trends in Student Aid: 1983 to 1993.* New York: College Entrance Examination Board, 1993.

"College Savings and Prepayment Plans." *Capital Ideas,* 1988, 2 (3–4), 1–15.

Commission on Independent College and Universities. *New York's Future: The Vital Partnership.* Albany, N.Y.: Commission on Independent Colleges and Universities, 1992.

Dowling, E., and Scannell, J. "Managing Enrollment in a Competitive, Financially Constrained Environment." In *Working Together: Cooperation Between the Admission and Financial Aid Offices.* New York: College Board, 1993.

Finn, C. "Why Do We Need Financial Aid?" Unpublished paper presented at four regional College Scholarship Service 30th Anniversary Colloquia, 1984.

Frances, C., and Morning, C. "Access to College: The Role of Family Income." *Higher Education Extension Service Review,* 1993, 4 (4), 1–11.

Jaschik, S. "One Percent Decline in State Support for College Thought to Be First Two-Year Drop Ever." *Chronicle of Higher Education,* Oct. 21, 1992, pp. A21, A26.

Kolderie, T., Lerman, R., and Moskos, C. "Educating America: A New Compact for Opportunity and Citizenship." In W. Marshall and M. Schram (eds.), *Mandate for Change.* New York: Berkley Books, 1992.

Leslie, L., and Brinkman, P. *The Economic Value of Higher Education.* New York: American Council on Education and Macmillan, 1988.

McPherson, M., and Schapiro, M. *Keeping College Affordable.* New York: Brookings Institute, 1991.

Moll, R. "The Scramble to Get the New Class." *Change,* Mar./Apr. 1994, pp. 11–17.

National Association of College Admission Counselors. *Membership Directory and Association Policies 1994–1995.* Alexandria, Va.: National Association of College Admission Counselors, 1994.

Postsecondary Education Opportunity (staff). "State Colleges' and Universities' Share of State Government Expenditures Declined Further in 1992." *Postsecondary Education Opportunity,* June 1994, 24, 1–15.

Regents Commission on Higher Education. *Sharing the Challenge.* Albany: New York State Education Department, 1993.

Sanoff, A. "Almost Anything Goes." *U.S. News and World Report,* Oct. 11, 1993, pp. 93–96.

Scannell, J. *The Effect of Financial Aid Policies on Admission and Enrollment.* New York: College Entrance Examination Board, 1992.

"Tuition Trap." *Washington Post,* June 2, 1994, p. A22.

KATHY A. KURZ is associate vice president for enrollment, placement, alumni relations, and development at the University of Rochester.

The integration of admissions and financial aid operations with the rest of the campus is a key element in the success of the college or university.

Integrating Admissions and Financial Aid with the Rest of the Campus

David M. Borus

This chapter deals with the integration of functions in a college, explaining both how to think about integration and the specific forms it might take. Thus, we move from a description of the two traditional and primary components of enrollment management services—admissions recruitment and financial aid—to discussion of their integration into the rest of the campus. The importance of overarching campus goals is central, and it follows that many different offices and sectors necessarily cooperate to create sound enrollment management. The student affairs component is key. Two examples of coordinated management clarify the concept of coordination.

How to Think About Integration of Functions

Chapters Two and Three describe the two cornerstones of enrollment management: the attraction (recruitment) of students to the campus and the management of the financial aid function to support enrollment goals in the context of the institutional philosophy, mission, and budget. Clearly, what were once routine and perhaps minor campus functions have now become exceedingly important and complex operations. Admissions work no longer is merely a reaction to student inquiries about a college, but an aggressive, sophisticated, on-going activity. Financial aid is no longer a charitable student service for a small portion of the student body, but a complex business enterprise, heavily dependent on resources from federal and state governments and institutional coffers. Recruitment and admission activity reach beyond merely informing prospective students and their parents about the college's offerings. Both admissions and financial aid offices are involved with students and families

New Directions for Student Services, no. 71, Fall 1995   © Jossey-Bass Publishers   43 well before enrollment decisions are made, and financial aid's role continues during the years of enrollment, and often long after graduation.

To be sure, admissions and financial aid are the base partnership in enrollment management, but institutions that wish to manage their enrollments in order to achieve stability and predictability have expanded this partnership across the campus. All functions that support stable enrollment must be integrated.

Marketing a college and serving its students well are not simple propositions. Dehne, Brodigan, and Topping (1991, p. 8) present a typology of services provided by organizations, and point out that virtually all are provided by a residential educational institution.

> Your college may run an infirmary, own vans for transportation, run several dining halls, have janitorial service, operate a theater and a radio station, and offer insurance and banking services. Because colleges embrace numerous areas of service, marketing the college is more complex than providing a single service called "a college education." Marketing success may rest as much with the quality of the food and the cleanliness of the buildings as it does with a contingent of scholar-teachers.

Interestingly, what is now a twenty-year-old concept, the coordination of purpose and function of key offices in order to produce high-quality services with efficient use of resources to achieve the desired number and mix of students, can be viewed as a precursor of the quality management movement that has entered higher education. Total quality management, continuous quality improvement, and other variations of the process-oriented theory, which stresses a cross-functional team approach, are aimed at improved service to students (Marchese, 1993). At the heart of the quality movement is the assumption that efforts that improve efficiency in the delivery of necessary services and reduce redundancy of effort and expense can most readily occur when offices and individuals in the institution work together toward common goals, a fundamental concept in ensuring adequate enrollments in a college or university.

Agreeing on Goals

Virtually every tract on management begins by exhorting the reader to assemble his or her group and set goals. As trite as that notion may seem, it is vitally important if an institution is to manage its enrollments. Without mutually agreed-on goals, the organization's units will operate at cross-purposes and risk dissipating resources and creating internal conflicts. Such behavior is likely to foster enrollment mismanagement and loss of students. Institutions, not just admission and financial aid offices, need to agree on which characteristics they desire most in their student bodies and how they are going to achieve and maintain the enrollment of students who possess those characteristics.

For example, what is the desired balance between quality and diversity? It might be easier to run a recruitment program that seeks students similar to one another, and it clearly would be simpler to manage student services if students were more homogeneous. However, the institution might value or need diversity—in ethnicity, age, socioeconomic status, academic interests, willingness to attend evening classes, and so forth. Similarly, the institution might value an international flavor and seek to enroll foreign students, or more pragmatically might need to augment its domestic enrollments with an infusion of foreign citizens. Diversity and quality certainly need not be opposites, but an institution might need to define quality differently from traditional ways as it seeks increased campus diversity.

In defining goals, institutional leaders also need to understand and articulate the balance they wish to achieve between rigorous academic education in traditional disciplines and career preparation in professional subjects. The relative emphases certainly will affect recruitment, selection, financial aid, advising, co-curricular activities, and numerous other activities that influence enrollment management.

A final example of the need to clarify institutional goals is the institution's determination of its geographical reach. Services will differ greatly on a campus that is mainly (and deliberately) local or regional in its student body and one that is intentionally national or international. Institutions that tout their internationalization often do not understand what resources they need to recruit, admit, and support students from overseas. Consequently, international students on such a campus might transfer after a short stay because the institution has not properly defined its goal of internationalization and established practices of enrollment management designed to achieve that goal.

Administrators, particularly those in student affairs who best know their students' characteristics and needs, can help or even lead the campus into more precision about its goals and how to accomplish them. This task should not be left only to admission and financial aid officers or those to whom they report.

Primary Partnership: Admissions and Financial Aid

One observer (Graff, 1986, p. 89) maintains that "most institutions remain a collection of fiefdoms with little focus or coordination: each office must serve while at the same time demanding service from others. . . . Moving such a feudal organism . . . is an Arthurian task." Overcoming such structural obstacles to the achievement of institutional goals by enlisting the support of members of the college or university community outside the admissions and financial aid offices seems critical, given the external challenges that face virtually every institution, whatever its primary role, standing, or focus.

The first and most obvious arena for the integration of effort and purpose lies in the admissions and financial aid offices themselves. Clearly, the objectives of these operations overlap, and both serve the population of incoming students (and their families) on which institutions depend for continued vitality. However, these offices may have conflicting objectives, too, with the admissions office wanting to use financial aid as a lever to attract and retain students and aid offices needing to contain the financial aid budget in order to enable the institution to have higher net revenue from tuition after financial aid has been deducted. Scannell (1992, p. 33) reminds us that these offices are sometimes faced with different reporting lines, with "admission reporting to an academic or student affairs vice president and financial aid to a finance vice president," increasing the possibility that the policies and actions of the two operations might become contradictory or confusing. Fears of such an unproductive situation have moved many campuses in recent years to institute variations of an enrollment management model in which both admissions and financial aid report to a single dean or vice president or, at smaller institutions, directly to the president. The way in which these offices interact with each other, as well as with other campus units, can be greatly influenced by the primary goals and focus of those to whom they report.

The primary admissions and financial aid officers should be part of ongoing discussions with chief financial and academic officials concerning institutional revenue and enrollment needs, so that they can jointly formulate sensible policies on the pricing of tuition and fees, awarding strategies, merit-based scholarship possibilities and limitations, differential versus equity packaging schemes, allowable flexibility in negotiations with individual families, and similar issues. Neither office can adequately conceive or execute appropriate policies in such matters without consultation with the other; to do so runs the risk of implementing costly and unwieldy programs. Financial aid practitioners also need to be actively involved in updating admissions office staff and other staff members on both institutional approaches and national trends concerning aid, so that staff and faculty can represent institutional aid policies accurately to students and their parents. In turn, admissions professionals must share their perceptions of student characteristics and concerns with their colleagues in financial aid and elsewhere on the campus.

Working with the Faculty

In *Creating Effective Enrollment Management Systems,* Hossler reconfirms what virtually every admissions officer has long known: "Student perceptions of [academic] quality are one of the most important determinants of college choice" (1986, p. 13). Litten, Sullivan, and Brodigan (1983) found that information about specific fields of study and the general academic reputation of institutions ranked just behind financial concerns as most important to prospective students.

As students and parents have become more attuned to the marketing efforts of colleges and universities and consequently more suspicious of the pronouncements of admissions officers, faculty have assumed a greater and more direct role in the explanation of academic information to candidates and their families. Faculty should routinely be included in such activities as phone campaigns to accepted students, open houses, faculty panels, and workshops, both on-campus and off-campus.

One marketing consultant and former university administrator asserts that "the faculty at colleges and universities can no longer afford to maintain the attitude that marketing activities are ancillary to their functions" (Neustadt, 1994, p. 22). The same author also reverses his equation, insisting that it is equally important that "administrators engaged in marketing activities are involved not just in the administrative but in the academic life of their institutions as well." Admissions offices that regularly share information with faculty members about the competitive marketplace for able students logically seem to have the greatest chances of obtaining a desirable level of faculty cooperation in the recruitment process. In turn, periodic updates from faculty on academic initiatives, departmental characteristics, and program changes can only improve the ability of admissions professionals to represent this critical area of the institution to the public competently, while possibly yielding the side benefit of higher campus visibility for the office within faculty ranks.

Admissions officers should also be involved in the discussion of curricular changes, new majors, changes in general education requirements, and new nontraditional student programs. Input from admissions professionals can speak to the possible markets for newly conceived programs and provide a wider view of how such changes might be received by students, parents, and secondary school personnel. Consultation with admissions and other relevant offices during the development of a new academic program will increase the likelihood that it will survive the inevitable changes or difficulties that arise. Such collaboration is a prime example of good enrollment management practice, drawing together seemingly disparate segments of the campus community to effect change.

Partnership with Student Affairs

There is virtually no work of student affairs offices that does not support enrollment management: housing and residential life, counseling, student activities, health services, career planning and placement—the list of specific activities and services is long. Not so specific is the social climate on campus, however it might be defined, but this atmosphere is also very important to students and affects their recruitment, retention, and future perspective on their college experience. Student affairs offices, if not actually in charge of this climate, directly affect it through their work. Indeed, Hossler's enrollment management systems model charges student affairs officers "to be more accountable for the ways in which they influence the attractiveness of the campus environment," for prospective students as well as for those already enrolled (1986, p. 25).

Admissions staff can provide valuable information to student affairs staff on the characteristics, abilities, talents, and interests of the incoming class. At smaller institutions, admissions officers often move beyond such general data to alert, within the boundaries of confidentiality, the dean of students' office to health problems, learning disabilities, handicaps, or previous academic difficulties of individual new students so that appropriate accommodations can be made. In turn, student life staff must keep recruiters informed on the scope and nature of available services and programs so that admissions representatives can respond knowledgeably to the questions of prospective students and their families.

Moving beyond the transfer of information, an ideal model will find administrators in student affairs, admissions, financial aid, academic affairs, and other offices collaborating to determine what students need or want and what the climate should be, and then working together to achieve those ends. It is not sufficient merely to be accurate and honest about how an institution is characterized to students; rather, in order to maintain necessary enrollments, campus officials must be sure they are providing the desired quality of education, services, and atmosphere.

If student affairs officers are responsible for assessing the outcomes of education at an institution, or collaborate with academic colleagues to do so, they should discuss their findings with admissions and financial aid staff. Not only does such assessment and subsequent communication help with future recruitment and selection efforts, but it provides institutional decision makers with a common base of information. A hypothetical, but not unrealistic, example is a gathering of college administrators to consider an exit questionnaire given to seniors. Respondents report disappointment in the degree of racial separation at their alma mater. They had expected better relations and more mutual understanding. Some indicated they had experienced more diversity and harmonious relationships in their high schools. Discussion among student affairs, admissions, financial aid, and academic staff reveals that, in their presentations to prospects and groups, admissions officers routinely convey a very positive picture of student interaction among racial and ethnic groups. They indicate that students have considerable choice in housing: they can mix or not; there are living units where students of one type or race can agree to live together, or they may choose other housing units where there is variety. Faculty comment that some of their minority students tend to be quiet in class and they wonder if their academic credentials are as good as those of others. An advisor reports that some majority students are resentful that students from underrepresented minority groups seem to get better financial aid packages.

What begins to emerge is a picture that reveals erroneous assumptions by several staff and inaccurate expectations by students. The harmonious and supportive environment the college is trying to develop is being undermined by some of their practices, such as allowing segregated housing. More financial aid, in the absence of explanation, is interpreted as favoritism when, in fact, it reflects higher financial need. Admissions is painting a racial picture in broad positive strokes without the data necessary for providing further clarification to concerned students. Faculty do not have actual data on the quality of their students; some are reticent to draw out quiet students.

Resolving this matter seems only to call for common sense and not to require an enrollment management solution. However, it is important to realize that such problems, left undiscussed and unresolved, may lead to attrition of students and, therefore, enrollment mismanagement. Without broad consultation and joint action, the problem, an ill-defined "dissatisfaction by all students over race relations," is likely to remain solely on the already overburdened shoulders of the dean of students or the advisor to minority students, instead of being more effectively addressed with urgency by a larger enrollment management team.

The perception of the quality of student life on a campus—the social and residential climate and the availability of desired services and activities—is a key element in attracting and retaining students. Helping to provide a high quality of life on campus is obviously the major function of student affairs offices. However, they and the admissions staff need to work closely together to ensure that the latter understand the campus environment and can explain it accurately. Reciprocally, student affairs staff can help in training their personnel at all levels to be helpful ambassadors when there are campus visitors.

One particular area of student affairs is becoming increasingly important: the career services office. Beyond the growing requirement by accrediting and government agencies for outcomes information, there is simply the need to be as forthcoming as possible to prospective students about how career planning and placement are handled on campus and, moreover, what graduates do when they leave. As college costs rise, career prospects for graduates will presumably grow in importance as a college selection criterion, and career planning professionals must be prepared to assist admissions by responding to inquiries and concerns.

The staff who manage student employment need to work closely with student financial aid, also. There needs to be good coordination in the job placement of students who have been assigned work-study funds in their financial aid packages. Wages for similar non-work-study jobs must be coordinated with the work-study wage scale. Where work-study funds provided by the federal or state governments are not sufficient, enrollment management offices (not just financial aid) need to work with campus employment offices to help students find work to help offset college costs. Obviously, campus offices should combine forces to help explain opportunities, limitations on work, realities about earnings, and so forth to prospective students and their families.

Office of Financial Aid: A Special Opportunity for Partnership

Graff presents an explanation of the multifaceted role of the financial aid officer that clearly demonstrates the need for linkages between this operation and other campus offices. He points out that financial aid work is part fiscal administration, part student service, and part enrollment and retention management. If the financial aid office is to serve these varied student and institutional purposes successfully, then it too must achieve a working relationship with other campus offices that share the goals of service and effectiveness.

As the costs of a college education escalate and the burdens on students, families, and institutions increase, financial aid officers find themselves working more closely and on a greater variety of tasks with colleagues in the various units of the university's business operations, especially those in charge of student accounts. The mechanics of the certification of aid and its crediting to the accounts of individual recipients are, of course, still vital procedures that take cooperation between the two areas, but a growing mutual involvement in activities such as loan counseling, debt management advising, assistance with payment plans and financing options, advising about personal budgets, and a variety of other financial services has increased the possible points of intersection between financial aid and other financial offices on many campuses. Indeed, a number of institutions have moved in recent years to a merged student financial services office concept, formally joining at least some of the functions once held separately in the two offices and expanding the range of services available to students through cross-training of staff.

The aid office is also a major player in institutional retention efforts, working with students and families to help overcome financial difficulties caused by shifting financial circumstances. They are also in a position to work with the student affairs office and student accounts on early identification of students whose financial difficulties may prevent them from maintaining the federal and institutionally defined standards for satisfactory academic progress. The financial aid officer is sometimes the first to learn of personal difficulties affecting individual students, and serves as a counselor and source of referral to other offices. International student advising offices often work with financial aid as well, on topics ranging from aid eligibility to obtaining appropriate visas and work permits to arranging for funding to cover unanticipated needs such as warm clothing or transportation home.

As college and university development offices raise funds for scholarship support, they often turn to the financial aid office, seeking assistance with stewardship obligations. Despite sometimes difficult restrictions, aid officers are asked to match students with donors and their funds, helping to increase the likelihood of donor satisfaction, which can lead to future giving and further scholarship support.

The various partnerships financial aid must form with other offices in the interests of student retention and institutional financial stability underscore a major concept of this issue: that financial aid is now a vital business function of the college or university, not a minor student benefit. Consequently, the aid office must be well integrated into the institution, not seen as only a financial unit, a branch of student services, or an arm of academic policy, for it serves all three of these areas and more. If senior administrators or the aid staff themselves view the office as having only one major function, or if financial aid is not truly a part of managing enrollments in the broadest sense, the institution will miss the opportunity to use financial aid fully in support of its enrollment goals.

Other Partnerships

As described above, admissions and financial aid intersect most directly with the student services, academic, and business functions of the institution in the pursuit of enrollment management. However, almost no division of the university is exempt from the overall effort.

Offices of public relations or public affairs have a number of overlapping purposes with admissions offices because the two, together and separately, concentrate on interpreting the institution to the public through publications, presentations, and contact with the media. To a much greater extent than formerly, public relations offices also convey and shape institutional image through explanations concerning pricing, cost, financial aid, financing an education, and value received. Both of these offices need to understand their respective roles clearly and agree on who speaks for the institution. Should admissions or financial aid officers talk to the media? Must the public affairs office always check with admissions or financial aid before giving out information on either subject?

The offices also should agree on nuances about the institution's image. Does it have a "generous" financial aid policy, or would a more accurate characterization be that the university is an "important partner with the student and family" in helping to finance a college education? Is the institution "seeking to modify its regional character," or is it "welcoming students from other areas while still giving close attention to its traditional clientele close to home?"

In particular, admissions should work with public relations to identify and target existing or potential markets, achieve consensus on the themes and institutional characteristics that should be featured, locate media outlets in communities with high recruiting potential, and systematize the supplying of institutional data to the many guidebooks, software companies, and others who wish to distribute information on and sometimes issue ratings of colleges and universities.

Public affairs officers, particularly those who have legislative relations as part of their jobs, should work closely with financial aid offices in lobbying or informing state and federal legislators about student aid and student financing issues.

Of course, publications used in recruitment and financial aid should support institutional themes. Public relations offices often have special expertise in expressing those themes, as well as in the design, writing, and production of the pieces themselves. Public relations and admissions officers must insist on the presentation of a consistent image, whether publications are produced in-house or through the use of outside organizations.

Chapter One listed nineteen areas that must collaborate in order to foster good enrollment management. Few units would be totally exempt, but if the list does not actually include the president's office, athletics, security, physical plant, alumni relations, and minority and international student advisors, chances for success are certainly diminished.

Avoiding the Gauntlet: An Illustration

The following is an illustration of an opportunity to use modern management concepts in pursuit of effective enrollment management. Many small colleges already have such a scheme in place and other, larger institutions, are converting to it. The collaboration involved is a good model for other kinds of cross-functional interaction, intended to solve institutional problems.

Specifically, on too many campuses, students run a gauntlet to complete their registration and business transactions. In order to register for classes or drop or add a class, they deal, serially and with growing frustration, with the registrar's office, the financial aid office, the loan office, the student accounts office, and, if they are trying to clear up a fine or penalty fee from the parking authority, library, or residential life, with those offices as well. The academic advisor, perhaps one of the most important people a student should see in the registration process, is overlooked along the way.

An efficient institution would first bring staff from related offices together to figure out what is going on in students' minds as they navigate this maze. Why does this difficulty occur? How would students design a better scheme? Then, the institution would examine each transaction for its utility. Do we really need to charge this fee? If so, do we need to hold up registration for it? Do we need a waiver form in triplicate? Do four people need to sign it?

Next, the institution would cut out as many of the steps as possible and simplify the remaining ones. Later, they might also decide to improve computer systems so that the former obstacle course is replaced by a few keystrokes. Some institutions, emboldened by their saved time and money and by increased student goodwill, decide to move the related offices into closer proximity or even to merge them. They make these decisions in the name of total quality management, helping students, saving money and time, retaining students, establishing good eventual alumni relations, or just being sensible. Whatever the rubric, the outcome is good enrollment management, and it illustrates how the integration of offices and functions can contribute to student satisfaction as well as the conservation of institutional resources.

Pulling It All Together

The integration of major campus functions pertaining to student enrollment and retention must go further than enhanced communication or even the collaboration of several offices. With admissions and financial aid leading the way, other offices and individuals must understand that the recruitment effort is essential to the overall health of the institution and the continued vitality and success of their own enterprises. For many in higher education, these understandings have almost become truisms, obvious facts of life in an uncertain economic climate. However, along with this acceptance of the importance of meeting enrollment and budgetary targets must come joint efforts aimed at increasing the mutual support needed to achieve those ends.

Admissions and financial aid are severely hampered when they are seen by others in the community as being essentially adjunct operations running parallel to, but not as an integral part of, the academic and student life of their institutions. However, spotlighting these offices or even assigning them relatively large amounts of resources is not sufficient. In addition, virtually all other campus operations, particularly those under a student services rubric, must be seen by top management as vital to the goal of maintaining healthy enrollments. One might go so far as to suggest that a test of the value of a program or new service is its relevance to maintaining enrollment stability. Unless resources are plentiful, it would be hard to justify new programs or operations that are only tangential to this high priority. Given the high stakes involved in the success of these operations at all colleges and universities today, it is crucial to agree on goals, identify the major players in achieving them, actively work on the partnerships, eliminate wasteful activities, and insist on coherence of programs and cohesion of operations.

References

Dehne, G., Brodigan, D., and Topping, P. *Marketing Higher Education: A Handbook for College Administrators.* Washington, D.C.: Consortium for the Advancement of Private Higher Education, 1991.

Graff, A. S. "Organizing the Resources That Can Be Effective." In D. Hossler (ed.), *Managing College Enrollments.* New Directions in Higher Education, no. 53. San Francisco: Jossey-Bass, 1986.

Hossler, D. *Creating Effective Enrollment Management Systems.* New York: College Entrance Examination Board, 1986.

Litten, L., Sullivan, D., and Brodigan, D. *Applying Market Research in College Admissions.* New York: College Entrance Examination Board, 1983.

Marchese, T. "TQM: A Time for Ideas." *Change,* May/June 1993, pp. 10–13.

Neustadt, M. "Is Marketing Good for Higher Education?" *Journal of College Admission,* Winter 1994, p. 22.

Scannell, J. *The Effect of Financial Aid Policies on Admission and Enrollment.* New York: College Entrance Examination Board, 1992.

DAVID M. BORUS is dean of admissions and financial aid at Trinity College, Hartford, Connecticut.

The wide-ranging functions of an admissions office create a significant institutional expense; enrollment management staff must be well-trained and flexible in order to accommodate students' changing needs and interests.

Fiscal and Human Resources to Support Enrollment Management

Shirley F. Binder, Caroline Aldrich-Langen

A fundamental assumption of this volume is the critical importance of recruitment, admission, and financial aid to any higher education enterprise. This chapter discusses the resources university administrators must marshal and apportion for these offices to perform their roles and deliver their services.

Attracting and retaining students is a necessary expense, not an auxiliary enterprise. This fact is well-accepted at private institutions that are tuition-dependent. However, public institutions are increasingly dependent on revenues from other sources than taxpayers. Many have dropped the term *state-supported* in favor of *state-assisted*. Many are looking to their students as a source of revenue, be it from tuition or fees. Thus, the entities most responsible for this major revenue stream—enrollment management offices—cannot be taken for granted, nor can the costs to operate them.

This chapter's first section gives cost categories and concludes with a discussion of cost containment and quality. The section on staffing explains the breadth of duties performed by these offices, indicates how staff upgrading is likely and necessary, and offers some ideas about how to think differently about the nature of staff and their training.

Cost of Recruitment, Admissions, and Financial Aid Services

The responsibilities of the offices of admission and student financial aid vary, depending on the size and complexity of the institution, the responsibilities assigned to those offices, and the degree of centralization. In a research-oriented institution with a large graduate or professional student

New Directions for Student Services, no. 71, Fall 1995   © Jossey-Bass Publishers

55

population, there may be multiple offices serving specific subgroups. Where the office of admissions is responsible for both undergraduate and graduate populations, responsibility for decisions on graduate student admissions is retained by the relevant departments or the graduate school. The resulting need to transfer paper applications from a central admission office to graduate departments scattered over a campus is being replaced by new technologies such as image processing. Although it is expensive initially, the saving in time and copying costs and the elimination of lost documents makes the potential for this technology very appealing. New developments allow the integration of document imaging with student records maintained in a mainframe computer system, thus making image processing adaptable to a large research university environment.

Separation of admission functions for undergraduate and graduate students has been the norm; however, recent efforts to consolidate offices in a cost-cutting effort have many admissions directors of large, comprehensive universities seeking advice on coordination of these functions. Student financial aid offices may serve the entire student population, or there may be multiple offices for undergraduates, graduates, and for each professional school. A third possibility is for financial aid representatives to be housed in professional schools such as graduate business and law, but to be administratively responsible to the director of student financial aid. This seems to be a very workable compromise. Consolidation does reduce some costs, but graduate and professional students may complain that their unique financial needs are not being met. Graduate student financial aid is also complicated by the need to coordinate assistantships and fellowships, awarded on a competitive basis, with need-based aid or unsubsidized student loans. Increasing federal regulations are so complex that central interpretation and oversight of compliance is virtually mandatory.

In any discussion of the cost of enrollment services, one must consider the size, complexity, and centralization of the institution. For undergraduate admissions, the recruitment territory covered must be considered. Does the admission office merely process applications for a college with virtually open admission? Are admissions and financial aid offices responsible for early outreach to underrepresented minority students in middle school and high school? Does the institution recruit simply through college night programs, or does it have a comprehensive marketing effort involving direct mail, on-campus programs, alumni activities, and development of publications and videos? Does financial aid place Federal College Work-Study recipients in jobs, or is this function handled by another office? Does financial aid train staff outside its immediate office? Do admissions and financial aid enlist other administrators and faculty in retention activities?

Answers to these questions affect the size of the budget of the offices falling under the enrollment management rubric and how they are financed.

Possible Sources of Revenues: Fees or Reallocation of Resources? Higher education exists under increasing budget constraints. Not surprisingly, governing bodies hunt for additional revenues and pressure operating units to try to match expenses to those revenues on some formulaic basis. In public institutions, where some state legislatures set tuition and where such income is inadequate to support expanding administrative functions, user fees are being sought for any service for which they can be justified. Admission application fees are an example.

The inadequacy and inappropriateness of application fees to support the recruitment and admission operation illustrates the narrowness of the definition of the function, as well as the complexity of the budgeting and funding processes. Institutional policy may limit the expenditure of user fees to the explicit purpose for which they are collected, such as the processing of applications, not the recruitment of students. Institutional policy may also mandate the limitation of fee amounts to the actual, documented cost of providing the service.

Admission offices often perform services not directly related to recruitment and admission, such as campus tours. However, those desiring the tour might be an elderhostel group or sixth-graders at a summer sports camp. The development office wants 200 copies of a promotional flyer or campus map; admissions prints these for recruitment and could easily supply them, goes the reasoning. But why should admission applicants pay for elderhostel tours or brochures for fund-raising?

A better example of an extraordinary cost is employee benefits, a cost that can add as much as 30 percent to salaries and wages in an admission office. However, a state might mandate an increase in benefits long after the application fee has been set in print. When these benefits continue beyond retirement, they remain a very high departmental cost until the death of retirees. Making admissions an auxiliary enterprise by trying to fund its operations from fees complicates accounting procedures and is a questionable practice.

Revenue from application fees fluctuates, depending on the number of applications in a given year. It is questionable financing to encourage admission offices to be so dependent on this variable source that staff seek inappropriate applications from even unqualified candidates or try to set up an elaborate scale of fees for every conceivable service they provide in order to increase revenues.

Another source, albeit minor in comparison to the cost of doing business, is the small administrative allowances allowed by the federal government on campus-based federal financial aid programs, such as Federal College Work-Study and Federal Perkins Loan Program. (At this writing, Congress is debating the reduction or elimination of campus-based federal aid programs, including their cost allowances.) The actual yield is 5 percent of the first $2,750,000, 4 percent of the next $2,750,000, and 3 percent for fund allocations over $5,500,000. It is easy enough to demonstrate that operating costs of the financial aid office, the work-study placement office, or the loan office far exceed such allowances. For one major public university, the actual amount of the total financial aid office operating budget of $1,700,000 supported by administrative allowance was only 20 percent for the most recent fiscal year. The percentage of students supported totally or in part by student financial aid is significant; approximately 48 percent of all undergraduate students enrolled in public higher education and 70 percent of undergraduate students in private colleges and universities receive some form of aid (U.S. Department of Education, 1994). Institutions must accept responsibility for providing a realistic operating budget for the financial aid office that ensures capable and sensitive counseling of students and proper stewardship of large amounts of private, institutional, state, and federal dollars.

Sometimes, outside funding sources can supplement an office's budget, gained from alumni contributions, concession profits, or administrative cost allowances associated with financial aid. Public institutions, with restrictions on how they can spend taxpayers' money, may become increasingly dependent on such auxiliary sources.

It should be clear, then, that admissions and financial aid offices cannot be funded from government cost allowances or fees, although such revenues might be a partial source. An institution must decide how important the functions of these offices are and allocate or reallocate resources accordingly. For some schools, there will be difficult trade-offs: they will risk less academic advising in order to provide more funding to admissions and aid operations. Other institutions, recognizing that their appeal is not centered totally in enrollment management offices, will eliminate or forgo introduction of another recruitment tool (a publication, videotape, an on-campus event, for example) in order to provide resources elsewhere that enhance programs for enrolled students, thereby strengthening the institution more fundamentally. For institutions wanting or needing to expand enrollment management functions, the most likely source of additional resources is not revenue enhancement, but reallocation from within or outside the enrollment management units.

Major Cost Categories. Regardless of the level of technology, personnel costs remain the largest single cost in the budgets of both admissions and financial aid offices. At the University of Texas at Austin, salaries, wages, and benefits account for 77.7 percent of the total admissions office budget. There is little reason to think that personnel costs will decrease. The growth of technology and competition from the private sector for technically sophisticated (or even technically literate) employees usually results in significant salary elevation, despite generalized assertions that automation saves money. In-house training by the central data processing unit of administrative staff can often satisfy the need for programming skills while providing an avenue for existing staff to upgrade their skills and become more valuable to the operation. Admissions and student financial aid offices will both be increasingly dependent on automation in order to provide a higher level of service with fewer staff resources. Electronic application processes, student record systems with tracking capabilities, financial aid packaging, and fund accounting systems are considered standard in even modest-sized institutions. Staff capable of using such systems effectively are in high demand.

Personnel. In both the admissions and financial aid offices, there are several categories of personnel.

Administrative: director, associate and assistant directors or deans, and program directors. The rewards for dean or director level, particularly in nationally visible institutions, are high; so are the risks (Moll, 1994; Sanoff, Morenoff, and Whitelaw, 1994). The National Association of Student Financial Aid Administrators (1993) listed $90,000 as the maximum salary for directors and a mean salary of $50,000. In an informal survey conducted in 1994, some deans, directors of admissions, and student financial aid directors reported salaries over $100,000.

Although a $100,000 salary in the mid 1990s is a substantial reward, it is interesting to note that, in one major public university, the total amount of student aid processed in one year was almost equal to the amount of state appropriation received by that institution for institutional operations, a very significant responsibility for which the compensation in the private sector would probably be much higher.

The College and University Personnel Association (1994) quoted the median salary for chief admissions officers according to five categories of institutions: all institutions, $49,536; doctoral institutions, $64,260; comprehensive institutions, $52,010; baccalaureate institutions, $45,000; and two-year colleges, $43,725. For the same categories, the median salary for the director of student financial aid was overall, $42,300; doctoral, $58,461; comprehensive, $45,874; baccalaureate, $37,000; and two-year colleges, $39,963. The median salary for the combined responsibilities of admissions and financial aid was overall, $53,693; doctoral, $81,764; comprehensive, $68,638; baccalaureate, $49,663; and two-year colleges, $42,283.

Professional staff, counselors, student development specialists, information specialists, recruiters. These front-line staff members are expected to represent the institution to students, high school counselors, and parents; provide college counseling, financial planning, and debt management; to be immaculately groomed, well informed, and charming; and, during peak times for each office, to work whatever number of hours it takes to get the job done. For this, entry-level staff with a minimum of a bachelor's degree can expect to be paid for twelve months of work an amount about equal to the salary received by an entry-level public school teacher for a ten-month contract.

A new interpretation of the federal labor laws at one major public university recently determined that admissions counselors are not exempt from the Fair Labor Standards Act and that they are, therefore, subject to payment of overtime for any time worked in excess of 40 hours per week. This direct contradiction of a universal practice could have a dramatic effect on budgets. It would behoove college human resources staff and directors of admissions and student financial aid to review job descriptions and responsibilities in order to avoid legal entanglements related to this issue, and also to transmit this information to the administration, making sure that the chief fiscal officer is cognizant of the budget implications of nonexempt status.

Clerical staff. The number and level of sophistication of clerical staff in both offices depends on the level of technology. Because of the cyclical nature of both offices, integration of the two in smaller institutions and nine- or ten-month contracts for some staff in large admissions offices may be a possible cost saving.

Data processing staff. The number and level of sophistication of staff included under the umbrella of data processing is quite diverse, depending on several factors. The amount and level of technology used influences the type of staff needed. The institutional decisions to purchase software and adapt it or to develop programs in-house affects the type of staff needed.

The location of data processing staff—in the central computing center or in admissions and financial aid offices—affects both the cost and nature of services performed. Achieving a reasonable and productive balance in the location of these important functions requires attentive consideration. Salaries for computer programmers, programmer analysts, and similar employees may exceed those for other senior administrative staff because of local demand and can cause salary equity issues.

Student helpers. Institutional philosophy again enters into the decision to pay regular wages, to hire College Work-Study students at a considerable cost saving, or to seek volunteers. Students can be very effective employees or volunteer workers in a variety of roles and are not only a source of inexpensive or free help, but also strong spokespeople for the institution as a result of their training and experience. In order for students to be successful in the pursuit of their education, as well as effective employees, supervisors must be sensitive to students' exam dates and deadlines for papers and reports.

Whether the adults involved in the college-going process like it or not, studies still show that prospective students are most influenced by their peers. Thus, students currently enrolled at the college or university are often effectively used in the recruitment process. The institution is fortunate if it can engage the help of a substantial number of *volunteers* who are responsible and reliable. Such students can be invaluable adjuncts to the recruitment process in leading tours, conducting telephone campaigns, hosting prospective students overnight in their residence halls, and making presentations. Sometimes it is necessary to pay wages to some or all such workers (through the Federal College Work-Study Program or via the regular part-time wages budget) in order to ensure performance and reliability. However, some institutions work hard to maintain a volunteer-help program, perhaps with some pleasant perks or rewards, so that there is no appearance that the positive attitude displayed might be construed as merely a duty for which the students are paid. At some institutions, there even is competition to land such jobs.

The amount of a student's Federal College Work–Study award is determined by the office of student financial aid. Placement of students can be the responsibility of that office or of the employing department. In some institutions, wages for students hover near or slightly above the federal minimum wage. Good personnel policy dictates, however, that individuals be paid according to the classification of the job they perform, without regard to their classification as student or nonstudent, part-time or full-time. Whether the student is employed through the College Work-Study Program or through departmental wages should not affect the hourly wage rate. The amount of the work-study award and the hourly rate dictate the total number of hours to be worked by the individual. Some admissions and financial aid offices avoid hiring students because of the need to ensure confidentiality of data. With good training and supervision, the savings are well worth the risk. It is also very good for students who, through work on campus, are generally retained at a higher rate, have higher grade-point averages, and tend to have more positive feelings about the institution and its administration than nonworking students or those working off campus.

Temporary workers. In these days of family leave and the lengthy procedures required for replacement of permanent staff, budgetary provision for temporary or part-time hires is important. It is also sometimes possible, during a hiring freeze caused by budgetary problems, to negotiate replacement of a vacant permanent position with a temporary hire. The seasonal nature of admissions and, to some extent, financial aid, invites the addition of a temporary-worker line in most budgets.

Operations. In addition to personnel, the second large area of costs are those associated with operations of the enrollment management units.

Communications. The methods and means of communications in the future are likely to change greatly. It is easy to envision interactive technology supplementing or even replacing current systems. Students surely will be able to use home computers to access the college's data systems to obtain information on admissions and financial aid. They will interact with the institutional data base, querying it for more detailed information on topics that interest them, including their own files, taking tours of facilities via the computer, and calling up photographic or moving images of the institution or of a procedure they are trying to complete. Staff currently in word processing centers might be transformed into managers of interactive electronic mail. Thus, the reader should imagine how some of the current and more conventional features of communications named below and now used in enrollment management might be transformed by new technology.

Postage. Most admissions and financial aid offices engage in mass mailings to students, not all of which can be anticipated before the budget is fixed. Admission materials and financial aid award letters must be mailed, often via first-class mail. Express mailing services such as Federal Express and DHL are often used to send visa information overseas.

Publications. Again, institutional philosophy is key. Is there a central publications office that designs and prints brochures, view books, campus maps, applications, and so forth? Is this the responsibility of the admission and aid offices? If so, is it done in-house with staff skilled in graphic design and desktop publishing or is it contracted out to an agency specializing in institutional identification and promotion? In any event, this is a significant budget item.

Videos, films, software. The phrase *In this electronic and MTV age* begins sentences that recruitment and financial aid staff can use to explain why they have or need to develop another means of communicating with students and families. Few institutions have been able to avoid the development of a recruitment film or video. Some can justify more than one: one to attract the interest of prospective applicants and one or more to help convert applicants to enrollees or to feature honors programs or other special opportunities. Financial aid and loan offices may develop videos to help both prospective and enrolled students. Admission applications and other brochures are now communicated by diskettes or CD-ROMs. There are various methods of developing and distributing these aids at high or moderate expense. Even offices that are under pressure to leave no stone unturned in the quest for students should assess carefully the cost and benefit of such features.

Telephone. The service options of telephones abound. Administrators should examine closely the many features and their cost and, importantly, the role these services should play in the overall management of offices. Toll-free 800 numbers for admissions offices seem to be an attractive feature, particularly for an admissions office that is anxious to increase student contact. However, such a feature requires well-qualified personnel (and, often, many of them) to respond quickly and accurately. It is difficult to refuse calls intended for other offices or students in residence halls; the receiving office may wind up paying the cost.

Voice-response and voice-mail systems are very useful. However, when it takes a caller many long-distance minutes to reach a live voice, or when the automated loop cycles back only to the programmed voice, the efficiency or cost-saving degenerates into an angry and frustrated public.

Sophisticated telephone sets provide users the opportunity for call-forwarding, voice-mail, conference calling, automatic redial, and other features. All of these have both their value and price, and offices should be certain that their staff use these features effectively in order to justify the expense.

Touch-tone telephone systems, now operational in many institutions, allow prospective students to perform status checks of admission and financial aid applications, determine availability of student aid funds without the help of financial aid staff, and obtain information about a variety of student services.

Travel. Does the admissions staff travel only in-state, regionally, or nationwide? What about international travel? Are financial aid staff expected to conduct financial aid information sessions in concert with admissions travel? Is there a per diem allowance or is full cost covered? What funds are available for conference attendance? Are resources available to bring high school counselors to campus or to take a counselor to lunch? These latter issues are of vital importance to the morale as well as to the professional development of admissions staff. Because travel is a high-cost item, institutions should evaluate carefully the benefits and consider whether other means of communication could be substituted, such as telephone campaigns, mail, or use of volunteer alumni.

On-Campus Programs. Because most colleges see a strong positive correlation between campus visits by prospective students and their families and eventual enrollment, they continue to support a variety of on-campus programs. These can be of modest cost (campus tours, overnight visits hosted by college students, afternoon programs using campus facilities) or expensive (paying the travel expenses of prospects or providing food, bus transportation, and insurance). Sometimes, summer camps or workshops for junior-high students are considered a legitimate recruitment expense. Decision makers should weigh the cost and benefits very carefully.

Data Processing. A major, growing category of expense is data processing. One expense is the purchase or in-house development of software. Another is hardware, ranging from desktop computers (which now are standard office equipment for most staff), to networked machines, to more major equipment, such as client servers or minicomputers. Staff to maintain the equipment and keep it up-to-date, to develop and debug software programs, to train other staff, and to represent the office to the computer center and other offices must be included in this cost category. In some institutions, there are chargeback systems from the central computer facilities to user offices for direct costs only, such as laser paper reports and mailing labels, or for use of computer time.

Chapter Six provides more thorough discussion of what data processing technology means for enrollment management offices.

Physical Facilities and Maintenance. The admissions office is the front door to the college or university. If it looks shabby or institutional, that is the lasting impression visitors will take away with them. A crisp, efficient, and friendly atmosphere in the financial aid office improves students' and parents' perception of that office. A long queue of students waiting for assistance in the financial aid office or at the bursar's window is a signal that something is amiss.

Research. Carefully designed research conducted periodically on the effectiveness of recruitment techniques, retention strategies, and financial aid policies could result in financial gains, both directly and indirectly. Such research may come from a well-established institutional research office. If so, the various stakeholders should be involved in the discussion of goals, the planning of the research, its implementation, and its analysis and applicability.

For campuses without robust research capacity, there are several services that can help, often at reasonable cost. The major testing agencies, The College Board and the American College Testing (ACT) program, have enormous data files of test-takers. With minimal effort, the institution can identify which students enrolled and work with the testing agency to design validity studies, assess characteristics of those who enrolled or declined to enroll, and make comparisons with similar institutions. These agencies may also be helpful with outcomes assessment.

Professional associations of admission officers, financial aid officers, and registrars may seek participants in national studies or may have off-the-shelf instruments, including student surveys, outcomes assessments, and office audit instruments.

A widely used study is conducted annually by the Higher Education Research Institute at the University of California, Los Angeles, in cooperation with the American Council on Education. The Cooperative Institutional Research Program is an attitudinal and characteristics survey used by over 400 colleges and universities and provides them data about their incoming freshmen that may be compared with subgroups of institutions (or all cooperating institutions). Some institutions have found comparisons with themselves over time very useful toward modifying programs in accordance with student interests and needs.

Research conducted by an extant or ad hoc consortium of similar institutions not only provides useful comparative data, but may be less costly because the expenses of design, printing, tabulation, and analysis are shared. Finding out that a competitor provides a better service or has a more positive image on major points than you have can be a cost-effective spur toward better enrollment management.

Not every activity lends itself to conclusive scientific analysis, but institutions should examine costly procedures in enrollment management offices critically, even if they are time-honored.

Cost Accounting. There is no pat formula that suggests the correct size of an admissions or financial aid office. Ratios of staff to students might be suggested as one way of determining size (and, hence, cost), but the functions of such offices vary considerably. Institutions whose students are primarily of traditional college age and who attend full-time during the day could have smaller staffs than institutions with many part-time students attending in the evening and on weekends.

In these days of increased costs, reduced resources, and heightened interest in the size, quality, and diversity of the incoming class, every admissions officer is concerned with making the most effective use of every dollar. Although addressed to smaller independent colleges and universities, *Assessing the Costs of Student Recruitment at Smaller Independent Colleges and Universities* (National Association of College and University Business Officers, 1989) gives a good presentation of cost accounting for recruitment that is adaptable to institutions of varying sizes and forms of control.

One measure of cost is the amount required to recruit one new student. One study reported that 76 percent of four-year public institutions spent $500 or less per student in recruiting; one-third of four-year private institutions spent $1,000–$1,500 per student, 23 percent spent $501–$1,000, and 37 percent spent over $1,501 (Williams–Crockett, 1993). In his article on enrollment management, Hossler (1994) quotes an Ingersoll Williams survey that found that "the average public institution spent less than $300 per matriculated student in admission office funds, while the average private institution spent more than $1,000. It is not unusual for a small private college to have an admission staff of 15 to 20 people or more (including support staff). However, it also is not unusual for a large public university to have a similar or smaller staff. Public institutions with such small staffs will not be able to provide the high-quality service and the individualized attention that will be required to compete successfully with the private sector" (p. 31).

Cost Containment and Quality. Higher education seems to be caught in a set of contradictory forces. The ever-increasing cost of a college education, static or reduced federal grant aid, new federal regulations requiring additional services and reports, and cost-containment measures by colleges and universities resulting in smaller numbers of staff with greater responsibilities all contribute to a need to do more with less. Coincidentally, the quality movement has been embraced by institutions; students and their parents, as well as all individuals having business with the offices of admission and student financial aid, have been recognized as customers of those offices. Thus, higher performance quality is sought just as institutions may be cutting out some of the resources thought to be needed to produce that quality.

Total quality management (TQM) has been implemented on a number of college campuses in recent years. Others are in the process of making a major commitment to quality. Associated with TQM is an activity called benchmarking. An innovative approach to the improvement of services in the face of cost containment was piloted by the National Association of College and University Business Officers in 1992. Shafer and Coate (1992) found that "TQM asserts that quality is defined by the customer, that it is less costly than non-quality, and that it is always changing—hence the need for continuous improvement." They describe benchmarking as "an ongoing, systematic process for measuring and comparing the work processes of one organization to those of another for the purpose of identifying best practices that can lead to improvements in operations and customer service. In other words, to benchmark is to ask: How well are we doing compared to others? How good do we want to be? Who's doing best? How do they do it? How could we adapt what they do to our institution?" (p. 30).

Kempner and Shafer (1993) give examples of how benchmarking can be applied to admissions offices. In one example, they contrast the number of days that five types of institutions used to process applications on average. The range at public research institutions was 2.5–21.5 days; at liberal arts colleges, the range was 3–17. In another example, they compare six activities or processes, including median applicants as a percentage of inquiries and median high school and community college visits per full-time admissions staff person.

Rather than trying to find one ratio between the number of applications for admission or financial aid and the number of staff needed, the authors suggest that benchmarking provides an opportunity to compare one institution with others with similar characteristics in terms of the quality of service. Once the comparison has been made, staff have the opportunity to consider changes in staff responsibilities or procedures or make a case to the administration for additional staff or system development.

Applying carefully the most applicable principles of TQM or results of relevant benchmarking projects enables institutions to contain costs and gain (or, at least, maintain) quality of service.

Higher education is a service industry with an intangible product, the value of which is in the eyes of the beholder. It is difficult to say when an admissions or financial aid office has produced enough service of sufficient quality. Even if enrollment management goals are met, families may demand more service. Also, staff may feel compelled to do even more for fear the competition will get ahead of them. Enrollment management staff need special skills of discernment to assess what is minimal and optimal service from their offices, both in the present and in the future. In essence, they are asking themselves, How much quality is enough? Then they must make their case to more senior administration and budget officers.

It does not seem likely that outside forces will permit the work of enrollment management to shrink as long as an institution wants to continue with all of its present programs and services. Long-distance calls are relatively inexpensive; airfares can be as well. Thus, families are likely to scout out college and financial aid opportunities even more aggressively and to feel comfortable demanding more of colleges, aware of the buyers' market.

The comprehensive nature of enrollment management, particularly as manifested in recruitment, admissions, and financial aid offices, causes it to be fairly costly. At institutions that are tuition-driven or are funded on a tight per-student basis, it is all too easy to strive for enrollment management at any cost, but this practice is no longer appropriate. Cost categories should be itemized and defined so that reasonable budgets can be established, but the utility of every program and the role of each staff member should be rationalized and justified. Even institutions that operate close to the margin of viability cannot afford careless expenses in enrollment management at the risk of academic programs. Good comprehensive planning with productive cooperation from key offices, no matter how large the campus, will most likely produce the most effective use of financial resources.

Staff: The Vital Resource for Recruitment, Admissions, and Financial Aid

Much of the work of enrollment management is labor-intensive, both because the staff perform a lot of transactions and because they spend much of their time explaining the institution to others and giving instructions about often complex procedures. In the previous section, we noted that 70 percent or more of the budgets of the offices involved may be dedicated to personnel costs. Thus, senior administrators must be concerned about what these staff are doing, how many are required to do it, and what level of performance should be expected. (A streamlined guide to selecting and training competent staff is R. F. Stimpson's chapter in Barr and Associates, 1993; also see American Association of Collegiate Registrars and Admissions Officers and the National Association of College Admissions Counselors, 1991.)

In order to think about these important questions, we can consider staffing issues under three main headings: the institution's mission, character, and size; key attributes of enrollment management offices; and skills required of staff. In addition, this section of the chapter explains the breadth of duties performed by enrollment management offices and the likelihood that upgrading of staff skills will be necessary in the future.

Mission, Character, and Size of the Institution. Few institutions would be willing to define themselves as mainly a business, a place where students come simply to acquire knowledge, where the interaction with other people is of nominal consequence. Very large institutions acknowledge that services and even instruction may be formal and somewhat impersonal because of the vast size when compared with small colleges. However, current management practices suggest a renewed emphasis on service, even at large schools. Small institutions, by contrast, advertise the personal attention they give their students as a key advantage, one that may even be worth paying a premium to obtain. Employees—faculty and staff—are going to provide the personal interface that makes the institution distinctive, that adds value beyond only providing information, formal education, or knowledge. The investment in staff at both large and small institutions reflects the character of that college or university. Senior administrators should consider what kind of character they want to convey and what investment is required to do so.

Small, personal, one-on-one, and *individual attention to students* are not necessarily good descriptions for an institution to use, just as their opposites are not necessarily bad ones for other, often larger, schools. Nor must an institution have a big staff relative to the number of students in order to provide high-quality services. However, institutional planners and office managers should be thoughtful about what services they should provide and what they expect from the students and families they serve. If the goal is to nurture and bring out the best in each student, staff must embrace these goals and be selected, trained, and evaluated accordingly. Recruitment staff need good listening and advising skills; they need to know their institutions thoroughly in order to explain them to others. The campus needs to have a cooperative environment where staff can easily call on others for help, rather than one where established structures necessarily partition responsibilities formally.

Other institutions, often larger ones, expect students to take more individual responsibility and to seek help when needed; the institution's nurturing behavior is more often a reaction to students' behavior. Here, the common expectation is that financial aid transactions will occur formally (via form letters, check-off forms, and touch-tone systems) and that personal meetings will be the exception. Prospective students may be entirely comfortable with large, formal informational meetings, as opposed to the friendly, personal interview offered at a smaller institution.

Staff on the enrollment management team should reflect the institutional mission and culture. Senior administrators responsible for enrollment management should be sure that the work environment fosters the performance desired of the staff. Wherever these offices are located on campus constitutes the front door of the institution for prospective students and their parents. Accordingly, students' and parents' initial encounter with outreach, admissions, and financial aid staff is their first impression of college or university life.

Key Attributes of Enrollment Management Offices. In Chapter Four, it was noted that good enrollment management requires supportive collaboration among offices. Additionally, recruitment, admissions, and financial aid staff must see themselves as team players with one goal: to convert qualified prospects into enrolled students, students who will remain enrolled.

Speedy Response Required. These offices deal with the public all of the time and must have the necessary location, space, ambiance, quality of equipment, and quality of staff. They work under deadlines that are self-imposed, imposed by external competition, or, in the case of financial aid, imposed by federal and state governments. Society's growing expectation of speedy response is abundantly evident in these offices. Before, prospective students had to compose, edit, and finalize letters outlining admissions, aid, or academic information they desired and then wait for a reply by letter; today, letters received by express mail, electronic mail, and fax scream out for attention. The demand for immediate response takes a toll on staff at all levels, and senior managers need to help define solutions to this fairly new dilemma.

Similarly, the growing use of electronic data transmission is speeding up response time as it is transforming the way certain staff work. Electronic transmission of the data from a student, high school, recommender, financial aid processor, or government agency directly to the institution's computing center or a staff person's desktop computer is already occurring and will be commonplace in a few years.

Cyclical Nature of Work. Another characteristic of enrollment management offices is their cyclical activity. Given periods of greatly increased workloads at certain times of the year, temporary and student workers often are appropriate. It would be incorrect, though, to think of summer as a low-activity time, as it once was. Financial aid offices are very busy with completing processing for continuing students and with loan applications, always heaviest just before the start of a term. Summer visits to admissions offices by prospective students have increased as families work this activity into their summer vacations. However, the specific functions of the offices vary throughout the year.

Need for Ongoing Staff Training. Enrollment management offices should maintain on-going training for their staffs. Financial aid staff need to stay abreast of many changes in state and federal regulations. Both staffs, with their dependence on modern technology, should emphasize current and relevant technical training. Also, these offices need to remain flexible. Their clientele changes over time, and these offices need to adjust, sometimes quickly if an institutional goal is to be as competitive as possible for students. To a greater extent than formerly, the public is telling the college and university what it wants the institution to provide. Although an institution is unlikely to eliminate the first-year English requirement because of students' demands, enrollment management offices cannot be so firm.

For all these reasons, it is valuable to involve existing enrollment management staff from all areas in the elaboration of a training plan, developed considering the various perspectives to allow the needed flexibility. Such a plan is more comprehensive and meaningful, and may foster a more stable staff. Because of similarities between financial aid and admissions functions (mastery of large amounts of detailed rules, regulations, and policies, and intensive clerical and technical activity), similar issues arise that might be effectively treated in joint workshops, training programs, and other educational activities.

Another rationale for involving employees across areas and levels in the planning process for staff development and training is the increased knowledge base such involvement brings. Consumers of higher education are becoming increasingly intolerant of multistop shopping. Aware of linked data bases, they want an institution to respond to their questions at one access point. In Chapter Six, a case is made for training the institution's staff to manage new technology rather than relying, in the long-term, on expensive consultants from the outside.

Staff Development. Finally, enrollment management offices should provide opportunities for professional and personal development of staff, as well as recognition of their accomplishments. Such programs demonstrate that administrators at the top echelon—or at the office or program level if a campuswide program has not been established—are interested in current performance in assisting employees to gain the qualifications necessary for positions higher up the career ladder.

Skills Required of Staff. The specific skills needed by staff in enrollment management offices vary depending on the exact area of work and the level of responsibility. One characteristic, however, is probably required of everyone: the ability to work with people, to understand their situations, explore with them available alternatives, and anticipate the important questions they neglect to ask. As important as this skill is, staff are expected to be mindful of detail, accurate with calculations, and aware of federal, state, and institutional policies and procedures. In order to perform satisfactorily and advance in the field, recruitment, admissions, and financial aid staff must possess these skills.

Leadership Skills. Senior-level admissions, recruitment, and financial aid managers need the ability to provide visionary leadership, to see well beyond the present to future enrollment trends, technological advances, and government initiatives. They need to have the flexibility to move from time-honored practices to newer and more effective ones. They need to be political activists, lobbying on behalf of effective student aid programs and admissions requirements. They need the ability to become "traffic cops" who ensure that all campus constituencies that are interested in recruiting and writing brochures are partners in a centralized plan that the public sees as a unified approach to marketing and recruiting. They need to be effective communicators, informing institutional planners what prospective students and their parents are saying and what financial pressures exist for new and continuing students. They need to solicit the latest information about new features, new staff, and new academic and student service programs. They need to be excellent personnel managers. Finally, they need to be financial analysts, keepers of the purse who can manage the resources allocated to their areas creatively and constructively.

In addition to leadership skills, managers and staff need one or more of the following skills and abilities; the amount and degree depend on their job responsibilities.

Communication Skills. Staff need to communicate with campus constituencies as well as with various publics (prospective students, parents, counselors, and other publics). The ability to write well is critical for basic communications as well as publications. Equally important is the ability to express oneself orally on the telephone and in person. Depending on the position, staff may be required to give formal speeches or extemporaneous and articulate responses in a question-and-answer format.

Public Relations Skills. The need for good public relations skills by the enrollment management staff is a theme of this book because these staff are the front-line troops. Additionally, financial aid and admissions staff often have to say "no." Thus, they need the ability to say it with finesse and compassion, accompanied by reasonable alternatives, and thereby gain friends for an institution, accomplishing long-term enrollment management objectives. The admissions counselor who coaches an ineligible prospective student toward meeting the admissions requirements contributes to the enrollment targets.

Research and Analytical Skills. Research and analytical skills are key for some enrollment management staff. Critical to institutional planning is information on marketing, future enrollment trends, matriculation rates, student budgets, federal initiatives, up-to-date minimum wage rates, validity and reliability of admission tests, and so forth. Enrollment management staff need to know where to find current and historical data relevant to their planning and forecasting and to be able to analyze the information in their own institutional context. Financial aid staff, more than ever before, must stay abreast of proliferating federal and state regulations. Staff must not only assess the applicability to their daily transactions, but advise or even insist that other campus offices, ranging from student accounts to the security department, understand and comply with these regulations.

Many staff in admissions and financial aid evaluate detailed records, often complex ones, and must be able to analyze, retain, and relate this information. The academic credentials of foreign-educated applicants (often in a foreign language), myriad styles of high school transcripts containing abbreviations and codes, income tax forms, trust documents, and the like are a few examples of the records that staff must understand and handle with accuracy and speed.

Marketing, Sales, and Publishing Skills. Every piece of mail, brochure, or flyer represents the campus to various constituencies, and a coordinated approach reflects well on the campus. Critical awareness of this impact and the use of communications professionals are key to an institution's public relations program.

Interviewing and Advising Skills. Although certain interviewing techniques can be learned, effective interpersonal abilities contribute substantially to admission and retention efforts. In Chapter Three, the importance of counseling as a skill is discussed.

Knowledge of Campus Programs and Services. Simply stated, staff need comprehensive and current knowledge of the institution.

Computer Literacy. Most admission and financial aid offices are now using computers for student data base management and reports, at minimum. As systems become more sophisticated, the skill level required of staff will increase. Less data entry will be required as on-line systems proliferate, because data will be transferred electronically from one data base to another, eliminating the need to reenter basic data (because of the advent of electronic admission applications, computerized testing, and electronic transfer of records from the high schools to the college's data base). A greater understanding of systems and mainframe functions, their component parts, and application software will be required. Already, most university job descriptions require some level of computer literacy. Although this literacy is often described as keyboarding or data entry, it takes on a new level of complexity. Staff must understand the data fields, the correct location of data, and the consequences of incorrect data entry, which can greatly affect an applicant's chances for admission or aid.

Although not all of the credit can be given to the intensive growth of computer use, one of the positive byproducts of advancing technology is that expertise develops across staff lines in such a way that support staff are called on to train professional staff and vice versa; also, support staff in one office train staff in another. The benefits that accrue diminish the borders that artificially separate functions and jobs.

Future Challenges to the Staff. Resources, including staff resources, for all programs in higher education will dwindle for some time. Will the technological developments that are revolutionizing the workplace dramatically change staffing levels? Will job skills change significantly?

There is a strong possibility that, given anticipated technological advances and computer literacy, problem-solving and people-oriented skills and abilities will continue to be of primary importance in the years to come. Of declining importance will be skills used by analysts who do technical reviews and computations. These activities will increasingly be automated and performed by computer programs. Many offices are finding that student demand for new or additional services absorbs any time freed up by better technology. Staff, aided by new technical features, will be able to quickly provide more comprehensive and accurate information on academic programs, applicable records policies, financial aid status, and degree requirements—all activities that enrollment management staffs are supposed to be doing in the first place and are uniquely positioned to perform.

Conclusion

Repeatedly, we have emphasized that the enrollment management staff are often the first personnel to encounter prospective students and thereby to create the first impression of the institution. Many, including admissions staff who may have many enrolled student volunteers and workers around them, continue to interact with students and families, even after initial enrollment. For these reasons, the quality of this staff and their ongoing training and development must be a continuing priority.

The demand for better and faster service is not likely to diminish. The frontline staff of enrollment management need to remain nimble enough to provide it.

References

American Association of Collegiate Registrars and Admissions Officers and the National Association of College Admission Counselors. *The Admissions Profession: A Guide for Staff Development and Program Management.* Washington, D.C., and Alexandria, Va.: American Association of Collegiate Registrars and Admissions Officers and the National Association of College Admission Counselors, 1991.

Barr, M. J., and Associates. *The Handbook of Student Affairs Administration.* San Francisco: Jossey-Bass, 1993.

College and University Personnel Association. "Median Salaries of College and University Administrators, 1993–94" (chart). *Chronicle of Higher Education,* Sept. 1, 1994, p. 32.

Hossler, D. "Enrollment Management in the 1990s." *Admission Strategist,* Spring 1994, p. 31.

Kempner, D. E., and Shafer, B. S. "The Pilot Years: The Growth of the NACUBO Benchmarking Project." *NACUBO Business Officer,* Dec. 1993, pp. 21–31.

Moll, R. W. "The Scramble to Get the New Class." *Change,* Mar./Apr. 1994, pp. 11–17.

National Association of College and University Business Officers. *Assessing the Cost of Student Recruitment at Smaller Independent Colleges and Universities.* Washington, D.C.: National Association of College and University Business Officers, 1989.

National Association of Student Financial Aid Administrators. *Staffing Models Project Salary Survey,* Nov. 8, 1993.

Sanoff, A. P., Morenoff, D., and Whitelaw, K. "Admissions Deans on the Hot Seat." *U.S. News & World Report,* Sept. 26, 1994, pp. 27–31.

Shafer, B. S., and Coate, L. E. "Benchmarking in Higher Education." *NACUBO Business Officer,* Nov. 1992, pp. 28–35.

U.S. Department of Education. "Proportion of Full-Time Students Receiving Financial Aid, Fall 1989" (chart). *Chronicle of Higher Education Almanac,* Sept. 1, 1994, 41 (1), 14.

Williams–Crockett. *Fall 1993 National Enrollment Management Survey, Report of Findings: Highlights.* Littleton, Colo.: Noel-Levitz Center for Enrollment Management, 1993.

SHIRLEY F. BINDER is director of admissions and associate vice president for student affairs at the University of Texas at Austin.

CAROLINE ALDRICH-LANGEN is associate director of admissions and records at California State University, Chico.

The increasing desire to use more technology raises complex issues of management and decision making, including vision, control, leadership, and cost.

The Driving Force of Technology in Enrollment Management

Joann B. Stedman

Enrollment management staff can make new tools enhance their capacity to provide better student services and even improve human interaction. Clear thinking about the possibilities of technology, careful revamping of business functions, and finding the right technology for the institution are essential.

New (and Newer) Technology Is Fundamental

Fundamental to the future of enrollment management is the incorporation of technology. Forces outside as well as inside the university are driving administrators toward technical solutions to management challenges. During a time when service improvement is a goal, the incorporation of technology causes a dilemma for the staff as extensive use of technology in a service industry is seen by some as too cold and impersonal. The challenge is to incorporate technology to achieve efficiency while controlling it so that it does not become intrusive in processes where customer interaction is at stake. Staff must also take into account that today's student is used to doing more things electronically; one could imagine a scenario where students interact electronically with enrollment staff and save their personal interface for the classroom setting. In the extreme, the following scenarios are technologically possible today. Readers will have many visionary ideas to add, but little change will occur without looking first at possible new ways to conduct business.

Scenario One. Bill was just hired as a marketing representative in the admission office with a famous, large private university. Bill is hot. He just graduated with an undergraduate degree in marketing and a minor in computer science. He loves computers and wants to use them to attract students to the campus. Bill is tasked with incorporating new technology into the marketing effort of the office.

First, Bill builds a data base of the high schools in the state and all those from which the college has received students in the past three years. He builds a similar data base for community colleges in a ten-state area. For each school, the data base includes a brief profile, the address, instructions on how to get to the school in case staff visit it, a history of the staff visits, notes from the last admission representative who visited, a profile of students for the last three years who have applied and their success rate in being admitted, their enrollment data, the test profile for the last three years of the graduating class of the high school, and the names of the counselors and principal and their alma maters.

Next, Bill builds a data base of information about the academic programs of the college. He includes information about the faculty, the major research being conducted in the schools, the names of the student services personnel in the schools, discipline specific scholarships, clubs and societies, honors, outstanding student profiles, and career placement statistics for the last year's graduating class in that school. Also included are sample schedules from students currently enrolled, and the school bulletin and academic regulations.

Next, Bill reviews the tapes, slides, and videos available at his university and compiles pieces of the various images together into a multimedia show that can either be projected onto a screen during a presentation or seen on the monitor if working with a prospective student one-to-one. He adds names, addresses, phone numbers, and Internet addresses of alumni admission representatives for every city where his college has such representatives.

Last, Bill designs an electronic application that can be copied to disk, filled out on-line, or downloaded to paper. He intends to use the laptop computer on which he is designing this system when interacting with prospective students in the field. Assuming that most students will complete their applications on disk, he will download the applications gathered while on the road directly into the admission and financial aid data base.

Now Bill is ready to go. He sees himself working individually with students while traveling. Because he is worried that the world has gotten too technical and is moving away from personal service, Bill sees the value in incorporating technology into his work to bring the student a more personally prescribed set of information about the college he represents. If he can sit with prospective students and their parents and talk about the various images of the campus and give them specific, not general, information about the students' intended field of study, it should help the college's image. Also, if he can show the counselors that their work together has results, he is more likely to get referrals of good students in the future. Bill sees technology as a tool to attract students, not an impersonal tool that will turn them off. He uses a computer to enhance what he knows and to bring better information to a prospective student, so the student can make a more informed choice.

Scenario Two. Imagine for a minute the enrollment management office of tomorrow. Assume that computer equipment is accessible to all. Assume that, in the new century, the manner of doing business by computer will be acceptable because the student of tomorrow has grown up with it.

The capability exists now for students to access multimedia view books, sample class lectures, campus tours, library tours, college orientation programs, and so on. Students will access from data bases information on colleges, financial aid, career opportunity projections by field, electronic forms needed for any college process, job opportunities in the community or surrounding area, housing, and more.

Record collection in the future will be much more efficient with electronic collection of data and electronic filing. No longer will high schools need to send transcripts, recommendations, or profiles by paper, and no longer will colleges have to file them repeatedly. Test scores and recommendations will be sent automatically to a student's electronic file.

Test administration will no longer produce such stress because students will take interactive computer tests at their leisure for admission and placement assessment, midterms, and final exams. Test security measures will have been established. Fees will be handled by electronic transfer and needy students will be given "education credits" that can be transferred electronically to pay for fees and books. No money will change hands.

Decisions, formerly made by staff, will be made by computer. The ideal class can be defined by the staff. Writing samples will be evaluated by text analysis programs and rated. Students will earn admission points for the quality of their academic record, community service, demonstrated leadership, special talents, activities and work experience, goals, and academic objectives. The computer will analyze the entire applicant pool's personal and academic profiles and recommend a combination of students that meet the ideal class profile. The profile can be adjusted by altering the ideal class formula. Admission directors can adjust for a higher percentage of science students, a higher community service profile, or students with more artistic talent.

The admission rating profile can be acted on immediately or only after all applicants are electronically reviewed. The computer will generate electronic mail notices from the director of admission giving the decision, but the decision will not be sent until the director has applied his or her electronic signature.

As soon as the admission file is complete, applicants will be given an admission prediction rating so they can begin to compare their chances of admission with those at other colleges they are considering. They may also provide more information if they feel the admission rating does not fairly represent their background.

Students will be able to get individualized information about financial assistance directly from the government. Once students give information about themselves, aid information tailored to their circumstances will be forwarded to them electronically. Information can be obtained on how federal financial aid works; sample packaging modules can be explored so students can see how the decisions they make will affect their long-term debt. Application for federal, state, and institutional aid will be done electronically and family financial records will be verified electronically. No more IRS 1040s! Institutional funds will be awarded to applicants and sent to them or institutions directly, based on the need rating determined by the federal government and the computer admission profile.

Registration in the future will be a very passive on-going procedure. Students will be able to register any time and for all four years if they wish. Students will consult on-line self-help advising files and can select and register for classes directly in the registration data base. That data base will manage classroom and facilities assignments, faculty assignments, class size exceptions, prerequisite analysis, add a section according to predetermined criteria, and give information on available class sections and required enrollment by permissions. Students will be assured that at the end of their sessions, their enrollments will be complete and their bills paid by electronic transfer. There is no need for preregistration or drop-and-add because students will be able to change their schedules at any time up to the point that bills are due. Yes, one can always drop a class according to institutional policy, but there will be a last day to add a course. Students can explore courses for the first ten days of class, if necessary, and then settle their schedules and bills without all the old rigmarole of refunds and supplemental bills. Students will register from home, a library, the workplace, at a kiosk, at their study abroad site in another country, or from airplanes.

The above scenario may sound too mechanical and impersonal to some. One must read the scenario again, this time imagining how the computer systems were prepared to serve to that very high level of efficiency and with such a personal feel that the student was willing to follow through the whole process electronically. Just as people now use ATM machines for banking, file income taxes electronically, conduct business by cellular phone, fax, and electronic mail, pay bills by electronic checkbook, and use electronic security surveillance in the home and car, students are incorporating technology in the way they do business. It is conceivable that some students will complete their college search, application, and enrollment process entirely by electronic means. Certainly, some will never choose to do so, and that human difference must be anticipated. The above scenario does not address in-person campus visits and other examples of staff-student interaction, which should be assumed as part of the process, but it does address the possibilities of allowing a higher percentage of prospective students to get at least an electronic tour of the campus. Many students now enroll without having seen any part of the campus, only the view book. This scenario definitely has implications for the international student market.

How does one get from the present office environment to the scenarios above? Should enrollment managers move in that direction?

Technology may be the force that drives enrollment managers to focus on the specific service objectives of the office. The exercise of thinking through the effective use of technology forces one to ask what the technology is being used for and whether use of the technology actually enhances the objectives or whether one is lost in the technology itself. Assuming some version of the above scenarios will be edging their way into enrollment management offices, what controls need to be put in process so that a balance is kept between efficiency, computer hype, and personal service?

New Thinking About the Use of Technology

Higher education is at an important crossroads regarding the use of technology. In many areas of administration, including student services, computer systems are aging. These systems, designed to mimic manual processes, caused the computer to become a repository of information about work completed manually in the office by staff. Today, in upgrading these legacy systems, the challenge is to avoid the simpler intellectual task of mimicking what staff are doing on paper. Rather, the road to take is the more demanding one intellectually, but more satisfactory in the long run: that of learning to use technology to do work that leaves people free to do other, more important tasks. In the case of systems supporting enrollment management, the next generation of programming should also use the computer to complete some of the work and thereby allow students to interact directly and more frequently with their own records. Ideal programming will also allow other personnel easier access to data about students.

Higher education is at an information-technology crossroads precisely because it is higher education. Colleges and universities are repositories of knowledge and are expected to know how to make expert use of it, in their administrative processes as well as the classroom. It only makes sense that admission offices be able to take the information given them by the applicants and use it to respond quickly, accurately, and personally to them. Counselors across campus, not just financial aid offices, should be able to combine data about students (grades, course loads, housing location, and so forth) in order to provide efficient help to those students. Thus, in upgrading computer systems, enrollment management areas should expect those upgrades to enhance their functions and services, not just substitute automation for slower processes.

There are many reasons for thinking more progressively, but one that needs emphasis is the accelerating use of electronic data interchange (EDI). Data bases all over the world are talking to other data bases. This technology speeds the transmission of information, but it means more information can be transmitted more easily. In turn, those exchanging the information have more to work with; as a result, their work can change.

Reasons for Thinking Differently About Use of Technology

Information and communication technology has been around for decades. Why the sudden pressure to incorporate it more comprehensively? Enrollment managers are being pushed to this new work environment because there are more external forces driving this movement than internal. First, customers expect it. Computer-literate students are eager to interact electronically.

Second, it is easy—or, certainly easier than formerly—to incorporate it. Commercial firms recognized the potential uses in education and have created products that make applying to college much easier by using computers and, in some cases, using electronic data interchange. Colleges that want to look modern use these products. However, in many cases, they merely download the electronically transmitted applications to paper, reenter the data, and process a paper file. Students will be quick to catch on, and enrollment managers, in order to avoid this snare, need to think differently about such use of technology.

Third, the government is quickly becoming automated, and the Department of Education and many supporting financial aid agencies are moving toward technology to manage their programs. The expectation is growing rapidly that colleges and universities will be able to transmit data directly to government data bases.

Other forces driving administrators toward more modern technology include the reduction in staff that resulted from economic constraints in the past two decades, the need to manage processes with more efficiency, the need for improved information about students and the institution, regulatory compliance (particularly in financial aid), electronic banking, the electronic information superhighway, greater public electronic access to library materials, and the technological capability of communication companies.

The presence of so much technological activity and change prompts the question, Who has control? Is the administration in control of the technology or is it just responding? Enrollment managers are encouraged to exercise or develop control over the technology and bring systems and staff computer literacy up to the level of skill expected by students.

Vision and Leadership

What are the first steps to gaining this control? First, a comprehensive view must be developed of what is to be accomplished in the next five to ten years. If vision is lacking and no plan exists that takes the institution to the year 2005, this plan should be developed first. Without a comprehensive picture of student service, application development, staff development, hardware configuration, growth plan, and connectivity, controlling the acquisition of technology or its cost will be difficult or impossible. This vision must be planned jointly by the senior administration from both the enrollment services and administrative computing divisions.

Reengineering the Business Functions. Most comprehensive plans today include a vision of running higher education entirely differently from how it was run in the twentieth century. New methods of information management are everywhere and the institution has but to plug in. Such change requires rethinking how work is delivered or, as it is called today, reengineering the business process to take advantage of today's technology. Reengineering is one of the most important concepts that can be addressed today. It is one of the few management fads that will probably become a useful tool.

Reengineering does not come naturally to people because it shakes the foundations on which they have always done their jobs. However, if new technology is to be fully used, consider reengineering first. Otherwise, plan to spend an enormous amount of money on new systems that produce the same work faster on more user-friendly systems or, in other words, expect faster, prettier, old systems! The customer will see little difference.

Another popular management fad of the 1990s is total quality management (TQM). Although it is useful in trying to ensure proper customer focus, good follow-through, and improvement in personal communication, it falls short of the radical change that is really needed. Hammer and Champy (1993) define reengineering as "the fundamental rethinking and radical redesign of business processes to achieve dramatic improvements in critical, contemporary measures of performance areas such as cost, quality, service, and speed" (p. 32). TQM provides an avenue for finding processes that need to be radically redesigned and perhaps stimulates change that is less wrenching. However, reengineering also allows for the giant steps forward that must be taken in order to reallocate resources and reduce bureaucracy. The redesign often involves increased use of technology. The spiraling cost of higher education is causing the product to be priced out of reach of the customer. Although it can be argued that technology contributes to that cost, if properly administered, technology can improve present cost ratios. One senior vice president of a major private university said, "The only way you could conceivably save money on a project that involves the purchase of technology is if you first consider business process reengineering" (Harvey J. Stedman, personal communication, 1994).

One of the largest mistakes made in using technology or buying applications is a lack of understanding of what problem is being solved. Problems must be sorted into proper categories for solution. During analysis, problems will be encountered in organizational structure, policy, process, procedure, tradition, personnel, leadership, information, finance, technology, vision, and politics. New systems cannot solve most of these problems, but many of these problems must be solved so that systems can be built. All will have to be addressed simultaneously.

Leadership. There is no substitute for competent leadership where technology is concerned. Case studies abound that point to endless redoing of systems, duplication of spending, and failed projects. In most cases, a trail back to the top can be found. Usually comprehensive vision, commitment, or high-quality decision making is lacking. Because senior administrators are not as comfortable with technology, they abdicate or delegate decisions to those who they think may know more. Those who are asked to make decisions often do not have the breadth of information, a true picture of budget possibilities, a clear understanding of the general direction of the university and its priorities, or the wisdom to make the best decisions. Senior administrators must take time out to become informed about this new world, guide their institutions through the sea of information technology opportunities, and establish priorities for spending and improvement in services. Fortunately, expert assistance can be purchased if it does not exist at one's institution, and this is a good place to consider employing a reliable consultant.

Changing Paradigms

The objective of any project involving technology should be to bring the service—in this case, education—closer to the customer. Over the years, a sizable bureaucracy has been built to handle the admission and financial aid processes. It is time to ask whether it would be more productive to focus more on the students being served (or sought) by the process than on the processes themselves.

Some risk is required to move to this new paradigm. As explained in Chapter Two, the college-going business is now so tremendous in the United States that it will be difficult to change the focus of everyone involved in the enterprise from the "getting in" to the "fitting in and succeeding" goal. Enrollment managers and their bosses would be taking risks to divert resources to the second goal in the face of traditional expectations about emphasis on the first goal. For example, if budget has been heavily invested in recruitment staff or brochures, it will be difficult to transfer some of that investment to more efficient academic advising. Management will worry; while they are waiting for the benefits of better advising to take effect, a long-term proposition, will their enrollment levels suffer?

One answer to this seeming dilemma is the view that the new consumers are not tradition-bound, that they can comfortably adapt to an efficient and effective system that manages their recruitment, admission applications, and enrollment, a system that has a higher component of technological aids in it and fewer labor-intensive human processes. The first step might be to talk to prospective and enrolled students to get their ideas. They might respond that they like the idea of directing their own ways through the process if given access to data in their own files, were told what to do to get to their goals, and were allowed to check on the progress of their applications from home. Focusing on how to make systems student-centered might reorient the entire process without financial risks.

Buy, Build, Share, or Borrow: New Concepts in Application Development

The most important question to ask when addressing the buy-versus-build software issue is, Who manages this service? Most packages are built based on someone else's concept of how to do the work. If one uses a commercial package, the process must be arranged around someone else's business concepts and ideas of how the package processes data. In today's world, the most important questions that are being asked are How can we manage our work or processes better to provide our customers better service? and How can we use technology to help us deliver better service?

No single enrollment services package is perfect for every higher education institution. Each organization provides its services in a slightly different manner; thus, if a package is purchased, modifications will be necessary. Many times, the modifications can take as long and cost as much as building a system from scratch, and this cost is in addition to the cost of the software package. Asking the staff to evaluate each feature of the software and to provide a list of the modifications that need to be written will give an idea of the cost, but even then, a modified package reinforces the old way of conducting business. Packages do not usually accommodate new transitions in business. Buying a package and insisting that staff use it as is greatly underestimates the resistance from the group that is being asked to change. Buying a package also negates the possibility that staff can find more efficient ways to accomplish their tasks. The smoothest transitions come within groups where the end-user group is consulted and made part of the decision-making team.

Computers can analyze data and support decision making in ways not previously possible. Combining these goals may mean building systems rather than buying packages because there are few packages available that use new technology and incorporate new business concepts. Most industry technical leaders are building their own applications, particularly because today's development tools enable staff to develop applications at such a rapid pace.

Until recently, buy and build seemed to be the only two viable options. Consider shareware, software libraries, or consortiums. For some reason, higher education professionals have learned to trust commercial vendors more than each other. While wishing to appear unique and competitive, many institutions manage their processes with exactly the same systems. Applications written at fellow institutions, made available as shareware, are often scoffed at, probably because most of the applications have been small and incidental to running major business systems of universities and colleges. The concept of sharing code is becoming more popular, as is the idea of collaboration among institutions, as the development of common standards and protocols becomes more popular. Tackling common administrative problems and adapting an application written at another institution is happening more often in higher education. The questions of support and documentation that inevitably come up with shareware are addressed by the consenting institutions.

In order to select the best administrative systems, institutions must understand what business problem they are trying to solve. Is it a problem of data integration, outdated or incompatible program languages, a nonrelational data base, or equipment or software diversity (systems not talking to each other)? Addressing the business problems and identifying a vision or direction is essential to the steps that follow.

Vendor Partnerships

System development must be a multifaceted partnership involving several parts of the organization (end users, technical staff, senior administration, data center management, facilities managers) and multiple providers of the technology, the vendors. Developing systems is as much a management challenge as a technology challenge.

The most unfamiliar part of the process for higher education administrators is working with vendors. Higher education administrators must understand partnering with commercial firms; not much gets done these days without multiple vendors working together. Because the vendors recognize that they cannot survive without each other, it is very likely a proposal will be presented that involves several companies' products. Such an arrangement can be advantageous. It may produce bundled prices and better maintenance contracts.

There are many vendors of many technology products, and vendors come in all shapes and sizes. Getting to know vendors and learning to trust them is important. If the project fails, the vendor fails; thus, they are usually as eager as the higher education staff for success. There are external, objective evaluators of vendor products who can assist with these decisions. Vendors can also provide references from other customers. In data comparison, the reference site should be roughly comparable in environment.

One vendor cannot provide everything needed. Multiple vendors will be involved as the system develops. Getting a clear understanding of how the various vendor products fit in is very complex. Even more complex is understanding how each product interacts with the other products currently used in the project. What alternatives does this vendor offer that are not seen in similar vendors? Is this vendor's business selling hardware, applications, development software, system software, training, consulting, facilities management, or peripherals? Because the college or university staff may be unfamiliar with the products, the project plan should allow time for informed decision making.

Service, technical assistance, training, upgrades, consulting, maintenance, long-range product development plans, open systems, product integration (with other vendor products), and growth of the products with this system are among the things that should be discussed with vendors. If good answers are not provided, ask more questions. Hasty decision making, usually the result of high-pressure sales tactics and year-end deals, may result in the purchase of products not needed or lacking the functionality desired.

Although company stability is one guide used to measure companies, some older companies are still working with old technology and cannot afford to abandon it because the research and development costs are not yet recovered. Company stability is important, but years of service in the industry should not be the only measure. How the product fits in this fast-growing industry and the company long-term outlook are also factors to consider. Investigate the technology the vendor is using to develop its own products and how its products will evolve.

Communicate with prospective or selected vendors frequently. It is only through good communication that a partnership can be maintained. Communication should be initiated regularly by both partners.

New Systems Project Team

The end-user community must be involved in planning and provide leadership for their part of a development project in order for useful new systems to emerge. A part of the system development equation that is often overlooked is the role of the end-user, the staff for whom the systems are being built. Today, however, they must provide leadership in the project because they are the ones who know their service best. They are the only ones who can decide how to conduct their work differently and learn how to integrate technology into their work.

The end-users must be the "business designers" and must interpret their needs clearly to the technical staff, who can in turn design the technical support for the end user's work. If the end-user does not take control of the project, the result will be faster, prettier old systems. Ideally, the project team will include people from all of the following groups: end-user offices that will be getting new systems (in this case, the enrollment management staff), the technical staff, senior administration, the project technical director, the project director for the end-users, and an objective observer.

The required time commitment should be made clear to this group and where the project fits in the priorities of the organization. Such projects will require many days of end-user time for a limited period of time while the system is being designed. This short-term time investment will benefit many in the long term. It may be necessary to arrange for temporary help in the units that are being automated because the extra work load may be too much for the unit to absorb. To develop a new student information system at the University of Ottawa, the end-user staff worked for several years writing specifications and finalizing definitions before selecting the technical platform and beginning the programming. Some staff were given release time to work on the project full-time.

Impact of Technology on the Organization and Staff

One of the many benefits of automating is the effect it can have on organizational structure. It is true that sometimes automation displaces people. Though distressing, anticipating that automation will eliminate some very low-level work and free people to do more skilled tasks can be beneficial. Retraining qualified staff has many benefits because they carry with them knowledge of the business. They simply need training on new tasks or processes.

Automation also creates jobs. Although jobs may be eliminated in one area, they will be created in another. The net result may be the same number of staff, but the nature of the work and the service and production level should change for the better. Consultants are available who can help assess the impact of technology and plan for the deployment of personnel to other jobs. Higher education as an industry joins many other industries going through this wrenching change.

The most significant changes to both staff and the organization will be brought about by reengineering. If successful in applying reengineering techniques, an organization can dramatically reorder its work and change the size of the staff. Leadership of a unit may change because fewer layers of staff may be needed for functions that are now automated. An organization is limited only by its vision.

Use of particular technologies may cause radical change. Image processing will have the most long-term effect in that it is one of the first major steps toward the paperless office. There is an argument among technical professionals about whether to skip over the imaging technology and go directly to EDI (electronic data interchange). Although the electronic transfer of data is on its way, it will be years before all paper can or should be eliminated; thus, adding imaged documents to the electronic file so that paper is eliminated as it comes through the door is a feasible first step. It is conceivable that, for at least a decade, student information offices will have to contend with data coming in all forms: electronic data, faxes, images, paper forms, and handwritten notes from staff. Information coming from other countries will be on paper for some time to come. Operations managers are hesitant to select one direction because, with such rapidly changing technology, they worry that a change now will look like the wrong decision in two years. Cost-benefit analysis of any technology decision should probably be measured in five-year segments because it is unknown what tools will be available five years from now.

Training

As explained in Chapter Five, changing technology has a significant impact on the initial training and retraining of staff. Staff training is one of the most important investments that can be made. Training must be obtained for each new product acquired, but the objective should be to develop, manage, and integrate one's own systems. Acquiring the expertise in-house should be the long-term goal. If an institution must rely on someone outside the organization to modify, fix, or run the system, a pattern of long-term, escalating cost is established. Several major hardware companies are moving from hardware as their product to service as their product. They are offering to do contract work at educational institutions at consultant prices, a significantly higher expense than long-term, dedicated employee prices. Building expertise on one's own staff is one of the several necessary steps needed for cost containment and improved systems.

If short-term help is needed from an outside company for installation, application development, facilities management, or consulting, transfer of knowledge should be one of the conditions of their employment. At the end of the contract, the knowledge and ability to run one's own system must have been transferred from the contractor to institutional staff.

Timeline

One of the most frustrating parts of developing systems is estimating the time it will take to complete the project. Accurate time estimates are almost impossible to assess because the entire combination of challenges that need to be coordinated usually is not apparent until the project is started. Often deadlines are set before the projects are even started. Senior administrators have been known to say "We are going to rewrite the student systems and will have them up for fall registration two years from now." How could they possibly know that? Identifying phases of a project and giving regular progress reports or setting benchmarks will take a considerable amount of the stress, conflict, and fear of failure out of the project management. Use goal-oriented terms such as *releases* or *phases* rather than *deliverables* or *deadlines,* which imply finished products done on a particular schedule. Administrators might be reminded that it took decades to perfect the systems that are on the market now. Although new technology will cut future development time considerably, it is not unreasonable to expect that, when adapting to new ways of conducting the office business, it will also take some time to develop the supporting system design. The end date should not be as important as developing the vision, both for the business design and the technical design.

Once time estimates are established, regular benchmarks of progress toward the completion of the project should be established and monitored. It is better to keep everyone abreast of the progress of the project and adjust their expectations as progress is made rather than announce at the expected end date that the project will be late. Optimism abounds in the technological world, and time estimates are often established on good data and assumptions that everything will go perfectly. Not factored in are staff changes, unexpected illness, end-user changes in requirements, and learning curves. Flexibility and patience are essentials of a good technical project manager.

A major factor that affects the timeline of a project is grandiose planning. "Idea management" may be the biggest challenge. When users are involved in the planning, the wish list of wonderful features may get very large, but some features may benefit only 1 or 2 percent of the customers and slow the development of the final product. Following the visionary planning, an essential next step is to identify the basic, essential features one must have to run the business, what must come up first, and what the desirable features are that can be programmed after everyone has the basic systems running on their desks. The essential components are ones that must come up when the system comes up; otherwise, the system will probably not be of much use to the end-user community.

Financial Analysis

It is surprising how few administrators know the cost of conducting their individual services now. They are aware of their budget, but rarely break out the cost of providing the various services of the office. Perhaps it is because higher education is primarily a nonprofit industry, tuition does not constitute the total income of the institution, and senior administration has not asked student services staff to cost justify the current service or service levels. Whatever the reason, it is not possible to evaluate the cost-effectiveness of the new technology if one does not understand the cost of the current operation.

When starting a technology project, it is important to document what goes into the financial analysis. Most technology projects are judged more expensive because the analysis was not comparable at the beginning and end. Also ignored is the value of improved services, better information, improved accountability, and improved product quality. Although it is hard to assign dollar values to these items, they should be taken into account as part of the objective of change. It is also important to be clear about costs that cannot be projected. When doing anything for the first time, there will be some unexpected cost. Most important is comparing the trading of one level of service for an expanded or upgraded same service (in other words, comparing apples with apples). If a service is to be radically altered, the cost may be unpredictable, but the possibilities of that are predictable.

Use of Objective Expert Help

What kind of expertise is needed to accomplish technology goals? Is the needed expertise present in the current staff? When adequate expertise is not available in-house, it is common practice to find an expert consultant to give advice and training, manage whole or partial projects, or help with planning. It is important to find someone who is objective at each step of this process. An outsider may see more quickly the steps that need to be taken. This advisor could help develop the phases of the overall plan and project a realistic timeline and cost of the project. This advisor should be willing to transfer knowledge to the local staff so they become more independent. It is possible that during the project, different kinds of consultants will be needed.

Consultants may also be employed to review proposals received. Proposals should be read not only for what they say, but for what they do not say. Very often, a proposal will give exactly what was asked for; however, later one learns that the proposal covers only part of what is needed. Anticipate as much of the total picture as possible and then ask an objective, knowledgeable person to read the proposals and ask questions. Each phase of the project should move one forward toward one's new goals and the proposals should clearly spell out how that will happen. The comprehensive long-term plan should be broken down into small manageable projects. Proposals should be requested for each of the project components that cannot be handled in-house.

Conclusions

Each part of the student information service chain works on links of the automation process. Whether motivated by forces within an institution or forces of the profession generally, professionals are constantly thinking about the next generation of technical assistance. Working independently, however, may defeat the goal of achieving an efficient integrated system. A vision of how the information system will work electronically should be discussed, and should take into consideration the full chain of processes and services. The chain includes high schools networking to colleges and colleges to colleges (through the Internet and using Standardization of Postsecondary Education Electronic Data Exchange standards), electronic inquiry and applications, electronic financial aid processing, electronic banking, automated loan processing, smart cards for storage of records, interactive voice technology for registration, checking of grades, automated transfer credit evaluations and degree clearance, worldwide links to study-abroad data bases, and so on. Understanding the big picture will help the institution assess its level of commitment to a new technological direction.

Reference

Hammer, M., and Champy, J. *Reengineering the Corporation*. New York: HarperCollins, 1993.

JOANN B. STEDMAN is a consultant specializing in end-user application of appropriate technologies.

This chapter expands on the major issues identified in other chapters, stressing those that are likely to be the most prominent in the next decade.

Enrollment Management in the Future

Rebecca R. Dixon

The past fifteen years have taught us that we cannot take our college enrollments for granted. Beginning in 1995, the number of students graduating from U.S. secondary schools began to increase, but it will be 2005–06 before the number equals the all-time high of 1978–79. The wake-up call higher education received in the early 1980s, coupled with other forces, has had the positive effect of causing serious examination of purposes and practices. Whether or not institutions use the term *enrollment management,* virtually all of them are much more attentive to the components of enrollment management: consistent and clear articulation of institutional mission, credible recruitment, comprehensive financial and financial aid planning, awareness of and response to student interests and needs, staff development and training, coherent curriculum, retention activities, follow-up with alumni, and many others. Most aspects of institutions have been reconsidered in the light of maintaining optimal enrollments.

The intentional concern for the welfare of prospective and enrolled students, even if it has occurred for self-serving reasons, undoubtedly has provided better student services. The goal for the future should be to keep the focus on students while making the adjustments necessary for the health of colleges and universities. To do otherwise would be to risk being manipulative or, at best, providing programs and services that suit budgets only, rather than their beneficiaries. This chapter summarizes the issues that will continue to be important over the next ten years and points to areas that will become more important.

Education Cost and Financing

This topic heads the list of anyone writing about higher education. It has a special poignancy for a book about student enrollments, though. It is from students, after all, that colleges receive a substantial amount of revenue. If

New Directions for Student Services, no. 71, Fall 1995 © Jossey-Bass Publishers students do not enroll or stay enrolled, they do not pay or have state capitation paid for them, and institutions lose revenue.

In the late 1990s, price trend lines at public and private institutions will grow closer, rather than continue to diverge. The discussion about the need for or the disadvantage of that convergence will continue for some time and thereby highlight the contrasts in the two types and, at the same time, the contrasts among the various subtypes of public and private institutions. The public may come to understand better, through this discussion, the difference between price and net cost (after financial aid is deducted). College and university officials should familiarize themselves with these issues in order to guide their own institutions, their governing bodies, and their other publics about the issue of who pays.

If public university costs begin to resemble private college costs more, middle-income families will be noticeably affected. Their costs will rise at the public schools, not offset by (much) financial aid. Already irate at not finding private institutions affordable for their children, they will feel the system has abandoned them. While legislatures and governing boards are sorting out the financing responsibilities, public institutions will tend to charge higher fees—for student services, for example—to make up for budget shortfalls. Consequently, families and students will demand more for the fees they pay or exemption from them.

Troubled by the cost of education even at public institutions, families are not happy when their children require more than the conventional four years to earn a bachelor's degree. Although closed classes are not always the cause, as opposed to student indecision or change of academic goals, it is clear that many state-supported institutions are under pressure to guarantee a degree in four years. Enrollment managers must explain the vagaries of choosing courses and majors just as they need to help academic units strive for adequate and efficient course offerings. Providing financial aid beyond four years, even if it is from noninstitutional sources, may mean less money for other students or higher loan debt for the extended student.

Payment for a college education has been shared with families and with the federal and state governments for the past forty years. As the century closes, some of the partners in the cost-sharing feel their capacity to bear their share is exhausted. Certainly, the federal and state governments are now near their limits in their willingness to pay, as well as their ability. The institutions themselves are still shifting or soliciting some resources to share costs with students through financial aid programs. However, the percentage of tuition revenues that goes toward student aid is already close to 50 percent at some private institutions. It probably is safe to say that the institutions and their donors are also close to their capacity to pay. That leaves only families or sources as yet unidentified to help finance education. Business and industry might become partners, as they are to a very small extent in postgraduate education. They might find it in their best interests to support students in an apprentice sort of program in secondary school and through one or more years of postsecondary education, but one could envision such an arrangement as operable for only a small portion of students.

Only a minority of families plan for the cost of higher education with long-term savings. Very few see it as an investment for their children as they see an investment in a home (increasingly, the costs are similar, particularly if the children attend private colleges). Additionally, there arises the possibility of inter-generational conflict over who pays. Many of today's parents, in their late forties or early fifties, want to be free of the financial burden of their children. They have postponed their own gratification for vacations or other goods, and they need or want to invest more for their own retirement.

Financial aid officers and other enrollment managers try to educate the public about parents investing in their children's education at the risk, obviously, of seeming totally self-serving. It should be the combined responsibility of all college administrators and faculty to encourage this investment and, more importantly, to make sure it is worthwhile. In the twenty-first century, college costs will make up a larger proportion of income and assets than they do now. Building public confidence in the value of your institution's education should be a concrete goal.

In addition to exhorting potential students and their families to make the educational investment, college and university administrators must provide more financing options for students. Loans will remain a major funding source and, undoubtedly, grow as a portion of the source of funding. Institutions may need to provide more loan counseling. They may need to provide long-term debt-servicing and debt-restructuring with their alumni, both to help indebted alumni meet their obligations and to help retain their loyalty to the institution. What happens after graduation is very important to managing enrollments.

Although it is difficult now to work your way through college as was once possible even for a full-time student, some low-cost institutions may be able to expand work-study programs to help in a substantial way to fund college costs. Student affairs personnel are familiar with the advantages and disadvantages of off-campus work experiences and will want to look closely at the portfolio of their institution's programs to assess implications for enrollment management.

Administrators need to understand fully the composition of educational costs and interact forcefully and continually with their colleagues about the relative value of programs and services. They should be familiar with the sources of financing, both direct and indirect, and exercise leadership in informing, persuading, or tapping those sources. The institution should define for itself the answer to the question of who pays and articulate that answer carefully to its various publics.

Government Oversight of Higher Education

During the last fifteen years, the federal government has demonstrated increasing concern about how higher education has conducted its affairs. This question promises to lead to greater oversight and perhaps intrusion. Another possibility, now appearing on the horizon, is a retreat by the federal government in its support of higher education at the same time that it increases regulation and oversight. The perturbations in the system of institutional accreditation increase vulnerability.

Is it possible or likely that some institutions, weary of government over-sight (or intrusion), would opt out of some federal programs in order to be free of such regulation? A short answer is no. It is difficult to think how even a wealthy institution could afford not to have some federal financial aid or the authority to approve students' eligibility for aid provided directly by the gov-ernment. The partnership between the government and higher education, how-ever stable or fractious it might be at any given moment, is likely to remain. For the foreseeable future, the direction is likely to be one of more government over-sight and, in constant dollars, less federal funding of student aid programs.

Administrators should not delegate only to the institution's government-relations representatives monitoring of state and federal action regarding higher education. Institutions should prioritize the support they want or expect from govern-ments and lobby consistently and strategically, not episodically or in a diffused manner, for the most important funding and for rational regulations.

Demographic Changes

Demographic changes for enrollment managers usually means the number of students predicted to graduate from American secondary schools (both pub-lic and independent), their age, gender, and ethnic make-up, and regional vari-ations of these numbers. Data from the National Center for Educational Statistics are helpful, but a source often cited is a 1993 publication from the Western Interstate Commission for Higher Education.

The decline in high school graduates that began in 1980 caused colleges to seek students from other sources and to improve retention of enrolled students. Increasing enrollments do not mean that the composition of students ten years from now will be the same as the composition fifteen years ago. Readers do not need to be reminded of the greater variety in ethnic background of today's stu-dents. Enrollment managers and their colleagues in student affairs should exam-ine demographic data and determine the relationship of that information to their own institutional characteristics. High-cost, selective institutions will not necessarily find more of the students they would prefer to have (financially able with strong college-preparatory backgrounds), despite the larger number of high school graduates. Public institutions, even those that remain low-cost and modestly selective, may find students with great financial need, with residual English-language difficulties, and with other weaknesses in preparation.

Clearly, there will be greater ethnic diversity among the college-age cohort ten years from now, with a smaller Caucasian component. A larger number of students from minority backgrounds could provide those student groups with greater comfort than they enjoy today on college campuses at the same time that college officials are called on to adapt their services and programs to be responsive. The composition of students has changed significantly since 1960 from a predominantly white, male population of traditional age to one much more mixed. Women, ethnic minorities, and retirees now generate more credit hours at many institutions than white males; increasingly, the student body is characteristically part-time, commuter, and older than twenty-four (Hossler, Bean, and Associates, 1990).

Those who plan admission recruitment already are aware that different ethnic groups respond differently to different recruitment activities. The need to understand that the various audiences an institution is addressing will grow and will influence staffing, programs, publications, and budget. For example, some colleges already have admission staff who are fluent in Spanish. There may be greater need for bilingual staff in the future, not only in the admission office, but in financial aid and elsewhere. Generalizations are not always applicable to an individual within an ethnic group, but admission recruiters already have noted that some are more responsive to personal interaction with the institution than to detailed written material. By contrast, certain groups respond in exactly the opposite manner. Adult, part-time students respond differently from the traditional eighteen- to twenty-four-year-old college student. One does not need to be a prophet to predict that multicultural programming on college campuses will only grow in years to come.

The percentage of high school graduates attending U.S. colleges has grown gradually between 1972 and 1992. Enrollment rates of eighteen- to twenty-four-year-olds have grown from 31.9 percent in 1972 to 41.9 percent in 1992 (Carter and Wilson, 1994, p. 44). This steady growth has occurred despite fluctuations in the job market. Although recent college graduates have difficulty finding professional jobs at the level they desire, there is still a strong tendency of young people to attend college. That tendency, coupled with the growth in absolute numbers of high school graduates over the next ten years and the interest by older adults in attending institutions of higher education, suggests that there will be more students and more varied students in the future. Looking further into the future, "soaring birthrates in the 1980s and 1990s will result in dramatic increases of high school graduates through the turn of the century. Indeed, 36 percent more babies were born in 1991 than in 1974" (Western Interstate Commission for Higher Education, 1993, p. 1).

Institutions should determine whether they can afford to maintain a position of appealing to traditional populations or whether they should modify programs, staff, faculty, support systems (financial aid, advising, and the like), and recruitment in order to attract these new populations. Because a greater supply of students does not automatically mean a greater capacity by them to finance a college education, institutions must find new sources of funding.

Curricular and Academic Changes that Affect Enrollment

Fundamental curricular changes in our colleges and universities occur slowly and infrequently. To be sure, there are occasional modifications, but the basic structure, driven by time-honored faculty preparation, is similar now to what it was fifty years ago. However, enrollment managers and student affairs professionals should consider the influence that curricular changes might have.

Also, there might be curricular changes these nonacademic personnel might want to raise with their faculty colleagues. Some examples follow.

In the last decade of the century, there has been discussion of institutionalizing a three-year bachelor's degree in addition to the traditional four-year degree. For those puzzled at this idea because it seems inconsistent with the fact of the explosion of knowledge, it should be noted that the three-year bachelor's arose as a partial remedy for the high cost of higher education. That is, the idea grew out of a need to manage (sustain) enrollments. Also, there is a difference between compressing four years of education into three years and reducing the amount of formal education from four to three. Administrators should consider this sort of idea very carefully. Not only does a three-year program affect the size of the faculty, use of facilities, staffing, and programming, but the concept raises the fundamental question of what a college education should be.

For many years, some students have studied college-level work while in high school. After enrolling in college, they may receive advanced standing only or both credit and advanced standing, depending on the college's policies. Even when they receive both, some elect to accelerate and graduate "early," earning a bachelor's degree in three years; others are able to bypass requirements and broaden or deepen their education because they start at a more advanced level on reaching college. The lines between high school and college will increasingly be blurred. College administrators and faculty must spend more time articulating their own educational philosophy and synchronizing it with secondary school preparation. Enrollment managers should be part of that discussion to make certain that it is coherent and defensible in a competitive environment. Accepting more credit toward the college degree from work taken while in high school (or from life experiences, for that matter) might make the college seem more attractive or less attractive.

Lines are also blurring between undergraduate and graduate preparation, between disciplines and subdisciplines. Faculty are wrestling with overspecialization, between their natural desire to excel in a field, where the amount of knowledge has expanded so greatly, and the need to recognize that institutions cannot sustain an infinite number of specialists. Enrollment managers must understand what students are seeking and help faculty understand how student interests must be considered.

Cost constraints will continue to produce sharing of resources among institutions of faculty, facilities, and courses. "Distance learning" is a term more often associated with older adult and part-time students, but it may become more common among traditional college students as sophisticated technology enables institutions to share, rather than duplicate, library holdings, course offerings, and even facilities. Enrollment managers must ascertain that their institutions are characterizing the situations accurately and explain these features to prospective students.

Students' interests and goals change and higher education often responds, if slowly and cautiously, with curricular or programmatic changes. Institutions have the responsibility and opportunity to consider appropriate and productive adaptations.

Measuring Outcomes of Higher Education

Mentioned above was increasing government oversight of higher education. More fundamentally, the public is concerned not simply about being able to complete a bachelor's degree in the conventional four years, but about what is gained from a college education. Regional accrediting associations now require demonstration of outcome measures. Obviously, a major outcome that must be measured and demonstrated is the acquisition of knowledge. That area is probably the responsibility of the faculty and academic administration.

However, there are other outcomes that must be defined and measured. Enrollment managers and student affairs professionals should work on this task together, harmonizing the various components of these indices. They should consider students' expectations on arrival, determine what characteristics students should gain or change during their college years, find a way to assess those characteristics, and, after students have left, follow up to measure longer-term outcomes. These measurements go beyond the conventional outcomes now readily available, such as test scores, graduation statistics, salaries, and number of job placements.

Managing such comprehensive measurement is difficult. No one is "in charge" of this longitudinal assessment unless an ideal enrollment management plan is in place.

Institutions must work harder to create a plan by which to measure both academic and personal outcomes of higher education because society, if not the government, will require information about these benefits.

Measuring Outcomes of Secondary Education

Educational reform as a new movement reawakened in the early 1980s. It is a major emphasis of the Clinton administration and of the states, as promoted by the National Governors' Association. One feature is the idea of outcomes-based education. Many adherents advocate the use of student portfolios as a basis for assessing what students have learned during the elementary and secondary years, rather than simply using grades and Carnegie units. They would greatly reduce or eliminate the external (and, perhaps, internal) reporting of such objective or sterile indices.

This prospect is daunting for directors of admissions, particularly those at large institutions. In order to process thousands of applications and to achieve a defensible objectivity of selection, such institutions are dependent on grades in denoted college-preparatory high school subjects, class rank, grade-point averages, and scores from standardized admission tests. It would be very difficult to redesign a selection process where quantifiable criteria were scarce or missing. One can envision that the only solution would be to assemble an enormous fleet of reviewers to read thousands of portfolios to interpret the content and level of courses studied and the nature of other experiences reported in narrative fashion.

In Oregon, outcomes-based education has been implemented to enhance the alignment between high schools and higher education institutions. Legislation enacted in 1991 mandates that, beginning in 1999, first-year students will be admitted to all institutions in the Oregon State System of Higher Education based on their demonstrated proficiency in six content and nine process areas. All Oregon secondary schools are required to begin offering Certificates of Initial Mastery (CIM) in 1996 and Certificates of Advanced Mastery (CAM) in 1997.

At a meeting called in January 1993 by the National Governors' Association, thirty leaders from secondary schools, higher education institutions, and educational associations addressed these issues, which were later reported in a monograph published by the National Governors' Association, *College Admission Standards and School Reform: Toward a Partnership in Education* (Houghton, 1993). No recommendations were made, but the participants did agree that debate on educational reform issues is still in the early stages. They also "concluded that the nexus between high school reforms and admission policies is only a small part of a broader discussion that is urgently needed among education leaders at all levels—elementary, secondary, and higher education—about the purpose and objectives of America's education system" (pp. 2–3).

College administrators should not just observe and criticize secondary education but should participate in the changes that relate to college entrance.

Effects of Technology

It is both fun and daunting to consider the effect of new technologies ten years hence. Enrollment managers need to make forward-looking decisions now about their goals and use supporting technology boldly and firmly. To be sure, admissions and financial aid computer systems perform many repetitive transactions, and because these transactions must occur rapidly and on a timely basis, they should be among the most modern and responsive of such computer-support systems.

However, campus administrators should be focusing on the student and on education, not on the enrollment process or technology per se. In the future, it may not be acceptable for prospective or enrolled students to have to call or visit several offices or sites in order to conduct business. It may become not just a waste of time, but counterproductive for students to ferret out college admissions and financial aid information by repetitive contacts with various universities and colleges. Just as travelers can call one travel agent to learn about all flights and fares to a destination, and obtain information at the same time about hotels and ground transportation, so may students expect centralized service with quick turnaround.

Advances in technology are likely to be as rapid in the next ten years as they have been in the last ten years. Institutions should exercise bold leadership to take advantage of communications and computer support to provide better services faster and more efficiently.

Staffing in the Future

Earlier chapters have talked about what enrollment management staff do or should do. The challenge for the future is selecting and training the best staff possible so that they are maximally productive and flexible. Institutions simply cannot add staff as new problems and needs arise, however legitimate they may be.

Removing barriers to their efficiency should be an on-going goal. For example, there is a growing movement to place all student support services in the same location. The office of financial aid, the registrar's office, and the bursar's office usually report to different administrators, but their work overlaps. Greater efficiency and better student service are more likely if these offices are in close proximity. If they do not all report to the same person, perhaps they should, or perhaps their senior officers need to interact frequently and productively.

Easy access to computer systems across office and divisional lines facilitates work and can reduce need for more staff. Sophisticated interfaces among systems, likewise, could have highly beneficial effects. Legacy computer systems may not be user-friendly because they are difficult to understand or use. Staffing needs—for both number of staff and training of staff—might be lowered with certain improvements to computer systems, or staff freed up by technological advances could be deployed to higher-level responsibilities.

Students will continue to use computers for more and varied purposes. Admissions, financial aid, and student affairs professionals will have the opportunity and challenge of moving more of their routine work to electronic transmission of data to students and thereby using their time differently in face-to-face contact with students.

In the near future, at least, it may be possible to hire more highly educated and trained staff. In fact, the tight job market college graduates face in the last decade of the century is a boon for employers. Because the requirements for use of more sophisticated equipment and software have also grown, the coincidence of these two trends, for employers, is fortunate.

Administrators should emphasize flexibility, service, efficiency, and building of skills in their staffs. Institutions should invest deliberately in appropriate technology to realize savings that can be transferred to better service or to other important activities.

Beyond the Near Future

Stated directly and indirectly throughout this volume is the belief that overt enrollment management has proven beneficial for both institutions and students. Even if colleges find a reversal of the supply-and-demand situation in the future, with students of adequate economic means clamoring for entrance, they will want to remain intentional about managing enrollments. Higher education is a public good with high investment of public money (through taxes), private funds, and time, and the public should be well served. A different market situation, where students are plentiful and eager, might reduce the need for certain activities, but a comprehensive scheme of enrollment management would suggest appropriate adjustments. In any event, the composition of students will be different, and enrollment managers must modify their management styles, plans, and programs accordingly.

U.S. medical schools present an example from the late 1980s. After a brief flirtation with declining applications, they rebounded greatly. Today, routine recruitment is no longer necessary, and resources have been redirected to other important tasks: searching for underrepresented minorities, developing new screening mechanisms to ensure better institutional fit, finding funding for students, and helping students to understand long-term indebtedness. The requirements of a new health care scheme, no doubt, will cause further redirection of activities. Enrollment management in medical schools, even if that term is not used, is here to stay.

A topic not treated at length in this volume is retention of students. There is no end to the amount of attention postsecondary institutions could give to this subject; it could be the topic of another volume. This is not to say that stopping out, dropping out, or transferring to another institution are to be avoided at all costs. However, a good enrollment management plan incorporates into recruitment and admission information helpful advice for students about reasonable outcomes expectations. Adequate plans for retention are important for both the student and the institution.

Finally, the enrollment management team, however it is made up, is well positioned to assess what prospective and enrolled students want and need. Additionally, they have great resources at their command. This combination allows, even obligates, them to project future scenarios for the institution regarding the size and nature of enrollments and how to achieve them. The team needs to have a comprehensive view of their own and the external environment and to communicate it clearly to other institutional leaders. Despite the very real pressures of daily demands, they are valued for their role as the prime source of revenues or students and, thus, are a major influence on the future success of the institution. Therefore, they should act with considered and intentional boldness to guide the institution in its attraction and retention of students.

References

Carter, D. J., and Wilson, R. *Minorities in Higher Education.* Washington, D.C.: American Council on Education, 1994.

Hossler, D., Bean, J. P., and Associates. *The Strategic Management of College Enrollments.* San Francisco: Jossey-Bass, 1990.

Houghton, M. J. *College Admission Standards and School Reform.* Washington, D.C.: National Governors' Association, 1993.

Western Interstate Commission for Higher Education, Teachers Insurance and Annuity Association, The College Board. *High School Graduates: Projections by State 1992–2009.* Boulder, Colo.: Western Interstate Commission for Higher Education, 1993.

REBECCA R. DIXON *is associate provost of university enrollment at Northwestern University.*

INDEX

ORDERING INFORMATION

NEW DIRECTIONS FOR STUDENT SERVICES is a series of paperback books that offers guidelines and programs for aiding students in their total development—emotional, social, and physical, as well as intellectual. Books in the series are published quarterly in spring, summer, fall, and winter and are available for purchase by subscription as well as by single copy.

SUBSCRIPTIONS for 1995 cost $48.00 for individuals (a savings of 25 percent over single-copy prices) and $64.00 for institutions, agencies, and libraries. Please do not send institutional checks for personal subscriptions. Standing orders are accepted.

SINGLE COPIES cost $19.00 plus shipping (see below) when payment accompanies order. California, New Jersey, New York, and Washington, D.C., residents please include appropriate sales tax. Canadian residents add GST and any local taxes. Billed orders will be charged shipping and handling. No billed shipments to post office boxes. Orders from outside the United States or Canada *must be prepaid* in U.S. dollars or charged to VISA, MasterCard, or American Express.

SHIPPING (SINGLE COPIES ONLY): one issue, add $3.50; two issues, add $4.50; three issues, add $5.50; four to five issues, add $6.50; six to seven issues, add $7.50; eight or more issues, add $8.50.

DISCOUNTS FOR QUANTITY ORDERS are available. Please write to the address below for information.

ALL ORDERS must include either the name of an individual or an official purchase order number. Please submit your order as follows:
    Subscriptions: specify series and year subscription is to begin
    Single copies: include individual title code (such as SS55)

MAIL ALL ORDERS TO:
    Jossey-Bass Publishers
    350 Sansome Street
    San Francisco, California 94104-1342

FOR SUBSCRIPTION SALES OUTSIDE OF THE UNITED STATES, CONTACT:
    any international subscription agency or Jossey-Bass directly.